FORWARD POETRY REGIONALS 2012
SOUTHERN ENGLAND

Edited by Helen Davies

First published in Great Britain in 2012 by:
Forward Poetry
Remus House
Coltsfoot Drive
Peterborough
PE2 9BF
Telephone: 01733 890099
Website: www.forwardpoetry.co.uk

All Rights Reserved
Book Design by Ashley Janson
© Copyright Contributors 2012
SB ISBN 978-1-84418-616-7

Printed and bound in the UK by BookPrintingUK
Website: www.bookprintinguk.com

Foreword

Here at Forward Poetry our aim has always been to provide a bridge to publication for unknown poets and allow their work to reach a wider audience. We believe that poetry should not be exclusive or elitist but available to be accessed and appreciated by all.

For our latest anthology we invited poets to write about a place or area they are passionate about. The result is a collection of verse from talented writers that, while varying in style, expresses and communicates thoughts, feelings and ideas about regions from across the UK to the reader. We are proud to present this entertaining anthology which showcases the joy and inspiration we can all draw from where we live.

Contents

Fe T Paglinawan-Gutierrez............1	Janet Larkin.................................33
P Parr 1	Lynda Hughes 34
Dugald Macintosh Thompson.........2	Thelma Glanville..........................36
Loraine Fagg 2	Joan Skinner................................37
Elsie Keen 3	Grant Meaby................................38
Susan Lacey..................................4	Sarah Robertson 39
Imogene Lindo 5	Jo Allen 40
Patrick Mannion.............................5	Royston Davies 41
Anne Cotton...................................6	Alan Dee......................................42
Frances Stubbs 6	Patricia Murray 42
Nathan Lemel 7	Michael Irish 43
Josephine Sach.............................7	Unbreen Shabnum Aziz...............44
Trevor Mercer 8	Gordon Miles 44
Gwendoline Woodland 8	Jane McCarthy 45
Edna Harvey..................................9	Elizabeth Bruce 45
J Little 10	Pauline Hamilton 46
Claerwyn Hughes 10	Peter Parbery 47
Marjorie Baker 11	Terry Reeves 48
Eileen Louise Baker.....................11	John Stanbridge 48
Irene Wainwright-Snatt 12	Lesley Gill....................................49
Christine Frances Williams..........13	Janet Miller..................................49
Lorna Troop 14	Meryl..50
Sheila Pharo................................15	Irene Briscoe 50
Robin Grigsby..............................15	Marcy Wilcox 51
Maddie Reade 16	Jean Smith..................................52
Joy Milligan 16	Bernard Doogan 52
Susan Ireland..............................17	Vera Brown..................................53
Stuart Springthorpe 18	Peter Rowe..................................53
Alma A Sewell.............................19	Sandra Gorton 54
Gillian Lewin 20	Brendan Whitmarsh.....................55
Margaret Deverson.....................21	Paul Schofield.............................55
Marion Tinkler.............................22	Robert John Collins 56
Brenda Casburn-Colvin 23	Margaret Bennett........................57
Barbara Towes............................24	John Bright 58
Alan Bignell.................................25	Margaret Gane 59
Bill Tapping 26	Gladys C'Ailceta 59
Chris Porteous............................27	Brian Gamage 60
Kathy Dickenson.........................28	Yvonne Golledge 60
Frances Russell..........................29	Leslie Dennis Pearce..................61
Vivian Chrispin............................30	Anthony Green 61
Barry.G.Randall 31	Jenny Williams............................62
David Skinner 32	C. D. Spooner.............................63
Pat Salisbury-Ridley 32	Andrew Stephenson 64
Sylvia Ash 33	Anthony John Russell.................66

Margaret Ann Wheatley	67
Jill Harding	68
John Pert	68
Leon Gould	69
Matthew Lee	70
Veronica Charlwood Ross	71
T J Schaeffer	72
Jimmy Hamilton	73
Jean Everest	74
Wendy Whitehead	74
Jim Wilson	75
Yvonne Chapman	76
William Greig	77
Maude Kiddie	78
Nola Small	78
Nikki Robinson	79
P Pidgeon	79
Sylvia Russell	80
Brian Frost	82
Stuart Delvin	83
Jane Finlayson	84
Elizabeth Jenks	84
David W Lankshear	85
Colleen Biggins	85
Judith Herrington	86
Alan Dickson	87
Val Bermingham	88
Ron Morris	88
Pamela Dean	89
Henry Harding Rogers	89
Patricia Turpin	90
Alan Compton	90
Brenda Bartlett	91
David Macaulay	91
Phoebe Carter	92
Mike Goddard	93
Alan Smith	94
Iris Davey	94
Naima Artan	95
Teresa Mary Street	96
Philip Clements	98
Vaughan Stone	99
Fredrick West	100
Pauline Ann Smith	101
James O'Grady	101
Brian D Ball	102
Thomas Baker	102
Lorna Tippett	103
Richard Leduchowicz	103
Sylvia Herbert	104
Patricia Fallace	105
Muhammad Khurram Salim	105
Doreen Lawrence	106
Margaret E McComish	106
June Benton-Wright	107
Susan Stuart	108
Kamala Dias	108
Valerie Helliar	109
Errol Baptiste	109
Margaret Davies	110
Chris Bampton	111
Margaret Lawrance	111
Keith Coleman	112
Christopher Payne	112
Jean Hayes	113
Jeanne E Quinn	113
Allan Bula	114
Una Chandler	115
Ann Dutschak	115
Chris Norton	116
Eileen Whitmore	117
Robert Main	118
Shirley-Patricia Cowan	118
Valerie Coleman	119
John McCall	120
Bryan G Clarke	121
Adam Campbell	121
Sheila Waller	122
Mary Joseph	123
Jonathan Bryant	124
John Leonard Wright	125
Elizabeth Zettl	126
Emily Hendy	127
Daphne Young	128
Liz Dicken	129
Sandra Brisck	129
Leonard Watson	130
Zekria Ibrahimi	131
Trevor Perrin	132
R Wilson	133
Miss Terry Thompson	134
Mary Jo Clayton	135
Elane Jackson	136
Roma Davies	137
Elizabeth Elcoate-Gilbert	138
Dorothy Morley	139

S J Kattenburg	139
Joan Heybourn	140
Lucy Carrington	141
Jim Wilson	142
Julia Eva Yeardye	143
Sandra Eros	144
Tony Crawford	145
Mike Cleary	146
Robert D Hayward	148
Doris E Pullen	150
Ruth Daviat	151
Margaret Nicholl	152
Phoebe Brooks	153
Ali Sebastian	154
Dorothy Fuller	155
Bill Looker	156
Irene Carroll	156
Frances Searle	157

The Poems

The Tree

It captured my attention this stunning tree,
As if greeting everybody a happy day.
Standing proudly at the foot of the hill.
When the children wander to and fro singing Jack and Jill.

Spreading its breast and trying to reach up the sky,
while its leaves are swaying gracefully as the cold wind passes by.
I can't resist my feeling but to stop a while
And write a poem with a smile.

Strongly grounded that neither you nor I can break the sight.
For this tree was designed to give passerby comfort and delight.

Fe T Paglinawan-Gutierrez

The Cornish Oak

The Great Oak stands upon the forest floor, his trunk soars upwards to the sky!

His branches touch the clouds as they fly by! For centuries his kind has been the heart of England's wooden walls – would you believe that he is kin to me – a little Cornish Oak!

I crouch upon a bank, my twisted roots clawed into poor and stony Earth.
My back and shoulders hunched against the wailing westward wind!
Blackened by salt and spray, my bark is coarse and sodden, lichen flecked.
Boughs thrust forward, branches stream out, twigs a mane of tangled hair
Etched against grey winter skies, I am a nightmare tree, grotesque, deformed.
Within my trunk are many rings, witness to many autumns, many springs
Although I'm very old and growth is slow, yet still there's life.
Days lengthen, sap rises, tiny pale green leaves appear, unfurl.
At fall, hard tight-cupped children, most stillborn but one or two survive.
They'll need to be like me, resilient, a match for this harsh environment!
Although no man shall ever tame me as the ribs or keel of some great ship
Yet ever symbol of this ancient land, inside there beats a heart of oak!

P Parr

HAPPY VILLAGES

Spring and Christmas past, the snows have gone
The trees are growing virgin leaves heavy in bud
Birds warming their eggs waiting their hatchlings
Fruit trees are blossoming, cornfields are filling
Days much longer, getting hotter, warming evenings
Blackberries, apples, pears plums, wheat and corn
Harvest time now from the trees and fields
Church festivals, fruit pies, cakes and vegetables
Autumn leaves brown, red, gold and yellow
The wind's creeping in stronger, leaves on the ground
Snow so white with crispness and so very light
Christmas time and lots of family cheer
A year has passed so very fast but still nice to be around
How lucky village people are beauty and healthy air
Let's all feel sorry for those who live in town
Passing to and fro from morning till night
No beauty there just shops, traffic and old street lights
With lots of fumes smelly cafes and stuck in traffic
With no fresh air and their tempers flare
O how lucky us villages are.

Dugald Macintosh Thompson

ISLE OF THANET

A beautiful place to live
Surrounded by countryside and sea.
As the seasons change,
The farmers plough the fields
Then the harvest is gathered in.
The sea can be calm or fierce,
Changing very quickly.
Children laughing and running around,
A peaceful retreat to find yourself.
We certainly do share,
A beautiful place to live.

Loraine Fagg

My Old Town

When I was young in Uxbridge many years ago
The Fassnidge Park was upkept and everything aglow
The Rockingham Park had rails round
No rubbish to be seen
No dogs were there to leave a mess
And seats were nice and clean
The tiny little grocers and little drapers too
Were all so very friendly and very helpful too.
There were tramlines running through the gown
It was such a lovely place
But now is all so modernised
And moving at a pace.
No dance halls for the youngster
Where all their friends would meet
Those day were very happy,
No fights were on the streets
Please bring me back the good old day
As I still remember them,
One penny in our pockets
Was just our Saturday treat,
On Sunday off to Sunday School
In our Sunday best
Then home for tea, with bread and jam
Is what we had to eat.
So please god help us through these times
And take away our fears
For all of those who suffer
And those we love so dear.

Elsie Keen

A Green Serenade

I see leaves tremble on brown dusty bark,
As a red kite rises high above the trees,
Then onto mellow meadows of pastures new,
Where cool grasses whisper softly to the breeze.

I see the sunlight rest on wooded glades
And a multitude of grazing on the hills,
Boasting bluebells and sturdy beech trees
And all that glows a magic into splendid thrills.

Hamlet towns nestle quietly by gentle streams
And bridges curve over and beside the pond,
While sheep and poppies grace the verdant valleys,
Where there is so much beauty way beyond.

I hear the cuckoo echo and the wild owl hoot,
Way above this breathtaking and idyllic sight,
Across silent rills and unblemished scenery,
To take this fond memory into the dark night.

Standing in the silence of the evening,
I become totally immersed in it all,
To hear the cadence and trill of birds,
Where the odd leaf may flutter in the fall.

All this beauty is a cameo pinpointed in one place,
And it sings with a voice that is so very strong,
As dewdrops cling like pearls to lacework cobwebs,
And all in a romantic green serenade of song.

– That is the true essence of leafy Bucks –

Susan Lacey

The Sea

My grandson had never seen the sea before. I chose this
Perfect heat stained August day. He reveled in the

Treasures of the shore. He delight in everything he saw.
And paddled in the ripples of the bay. My grandson.

Never seen the sea before. He heard a seashell echo.
Waters roar and sifted sand from spade to bucket. Play

He revelled in the treasures of the shore. I hoard for
Home. I told him not to stray. My grandson had never

Seen the sea before. I should have watched him more.
Carefully. Made sure I should have know that he

Would creep away. He reveled in the treasures of the
Shore. I knew before they gave up looking for him.

My grandson had never seen the sea before he revelled
In the treasures of the shore.

Imogene Lindo

Soul

The green grass fields of Paddock Road,
Lays pounds and Victorian homes,
When ye walk past in fields of grass
Keep in mind the souls of the past,
So I say never walk past in green grass
Without ye saying hello so your soul may pass.

Patrick Mannion

EBBING

At Teddington I waited on summer evenings for the tide to turn,
To release the waters of the Thames and let them gush,
Let them hurry home to the waiting,
Anticipating, greeting North Sea.

Forty years later as I listen –
As I watch –
The tiny Linnet trickle to the Lark
My memories are of the Waveney,
Deben, Stour –
And Blyth –
And smooth, decisive, regular, regurgitating
To the ardent ocean;
While, further south,
Our monarch Thames is waiting,
Mesmerizing and tantalising while estuarising,
Celebrating Nature's power to thrill,
Astound and strike with awe
All powerless persons such as me,
As forty miles and forty years
Are gone.

Anne Cotton

LONG LIVE LONDON

London's a land where Luck and Fortune smile;
A piece of cake the whole world wants to share!
A prosperous place; it holds the Square Mile
Where Bankers spin vast profits of thin air!

It holds Big Ben, St Paul's; each tourist sight,
The Dome, the Shard, the Eye, each will amaze.
Feet will wobble on the Blade of Light
And visitors will pay to come and gaze!

Fortune seekers flock here, chasing dreams.
To where the urban streets are paved with gold,
Until our city's bursting at the seams,
With people it can't reasonably hold!

It can't be otherwise! The reason why?
We live and grow – else we decline and die.

Frances Stubbs

Southend Pier

(An idyllic and spectacular retreat by coastline and River Thames Estuary)

Why? It retains quintessence of pleasures and scenery,
causes a rise onto enjoyment, rest or repose,
even entertainment, an environmental first.

Furthermore, the longest pier in the world
has mud flats hiding 'oxygen modules',
to provide old, young, sick or fit
with purer air than elsewhere.

With those view of Thames Waterway
outlines near or far.
Up to Kent coast; many splendid scene of the
Estuary and stronger glows of horizon outlines.

Not least are the beaches
havens for 'London Eastenders', seeking solace
for tranquility or recuperation from turmoil
and capital's rat race, an ideal holiday resort.

Truly unique with the air, beaches and
splendid view, this is 'London's seaside',

Evermore a bonus, the miniature rail line along the pier,
withal remembrance estuary's 'epic small boats'
At Dunkirk rescue and saviour.

Nathan Lemel

Colchester Castle

Britain's oldest recorded town was once burnt down
Dedicated to the god of war it became part of Roman law.

Camulodunum was once its name,
Until the Emperor Claudius used it for his fame.

Boudicca changed all that
Making the town completely flat.

Like a phoenix from the ashes rise
Colchester citizens now live with pride.

Britain's oldest recorded town it is said
Towards which the tourists are led.

Josephine Sach

DUNKIRK TO DOVER

Wind blowing summer breeze
Shells falling through the trees
Battle weary, but not beat yet
Home to England our sights are set,
Come on lads, it's time to go
Scared and tired cold and wet
It's home to England and not beaten yet
I would like to sleep and drift away
To be home in Kent on a summer's day
To see the sheep and field of hay
Cricket playing on the village green
Machine-gun fire to my fright, I try to hide out of sight
Little boat and great big sea England holds the world for me
All I love and all I am
I thank God, I am an Englishman.

Trevor Mercer

WALKS OF MEDWAY

Golden fields of rape
Glittering in the sun.
Green shoots of wheat
Breaking golden light.
Mist of heather on the downs,
A mix of wild flowers, stand tall and proud.
May flowers showing pink, spring and summer
Show a hue of colours.
Bracken and gorse, different shades of green
Bluebells, primroses and orchids amongst the woodland trees.
Birds in song with the sounds of crickets see insects crawl together.

The ponds alive with frogs, toads, water boatmen and frogspawn, all bright in the sun.
Sound, sight and smell a wonderful thing
Walk, ride, and relax whichever you choose,
Enjoy the countryside.

Gwendoline Woodland

GREEN, WHITE, BLUE AND GREY

Green, white, blue and grey . . .
Kent yesterday and Kent today,
Green, in this room, is for me
A window-hugging cherry tree.
Other trees round join in its dance,
An emerald hedge
Seems to advance
To join the wand-like tree.
Green, all green, envelops me

White are the cliffs that
Boldly stare
At La Belle France,
Just over there . . .
. . . Or so it seems from the Port of Dover
when I return from 'going over' . . .
Pale, proud, strong, defiant
Staunch and immovable,
Like some protective giant

Blue, oh blue, is Whitstable sea
On sunny days, when at their shiny best,
It matches the sky in bright contest
Equally azure, equally blessed.
Blue, when I'm blue,
Is a treasured prize
Where children build their sandy pies.
Margate and Ramsgate, Folkestone, Hythe
All share the blue that makes me blithe.

Grey sounds like gloom, but oh! I'm very
Joyful when in Canterbury,
Where the majestic cathedral's grey
Speaks to me of yesterday
Of tragic Becket and many a king
Near stalls where fresh-faced choirboys sing . . .
Whose notes to fluted ceiling wing
. . . Green, white, blue and grey,
Kent yesterday and Kent today.

Edna Harvey

Essex And London

This small part of Essex and London
Is soon to be showcased
Not only to the nation but around the world
Flags are unfurled
As the Olympic flame arrives
Hopes and dreams are ignited
As athletes prepare and crowds get excited
In this small part of Essex and London

As the swimmers swim and the runners run
Will the rain still pour or the warmth of the sun
Beam out to the billions who tune in
Where sports and culture merge
And patriotism takes a surge
In this small part of Essex and London

And as the Games draw nearer
The disruption becomes clearer
Roads to be closed and traffic diverted
Tenants join up to get weapons averted
From parks and rooftop
Any danger to stop
As some ask 'What's it all for –
Is it sport or war?'
In this small part of Essex and London.

J Little

A Wealden Storm In Summer

Chalky grey smudged clouds tumble expectantly over the Weald
Coppice, now and again, freckled by sunlight
From the seas beyond, glassy raindrops swirl
And joyfully, the wind twists watery rainbows
Showers tumble down valleys, then tenderly
Fields are softly bathed in mists and light.
Birdsong fluttering on the warming breeze.

Claerwyn Hughes

My Land

This, my land, this part of Cambridgeshire
The place where I was born
Travelling through the world I return
To my land, my home
My part is in the south I know best
A village full of history, a character of its own
My house is of course where I am safe and happy
But the whole place is still my home
The people I know, the things I do
Are all connected from day to day
As I travel on my way
My family live around me so I am content
Together with the beautiful surroundings
The woods, the meadows, the little stream
The birds singing their songs
The church bells ringing
Village events and happy time
All make life worthwhile, each day exciting
Young and old, joy and sorrow
What will come tomorrow?
Fear not this region, my land, my home
Will always be the best wherever I may roam . . .

Marjorie Baker

Hop Picking In Kent (1905-2012)

In horse-drawn bus from far they came,
To pick the hops in sun and rain.
There, mums with kids and dads so tall,
Had country breaks, enjoyed by all.

Their hands grew sore as they picked all day,
When evening came the sang the sores away.
It was a holiday for them,
Who could not afford a 'hotel gem'.

From way, way back to present day,
'Hop Picker's Breaks' are here to stay.
And then, to celebrate it all
There is a 'Happy Hopper's Ball'.

Eileen Louise Baker

The River Ouse And The Flecci

From trickling streams at Slaugham and Ardingly
Sprang the River Ouse,
Though its mouth has moved eastward
It still weaves and wanders through the county.
As it did when the Flecci came in longboats,
The men eager, the women anxious, children crying,
Bringing cattle, small animals and seed
And a few possessions, to this marshy shore
So different from the sandy wastes of home.

They followed the saltwater river
To a distant hill, now the town of Lewes,
And looked beyond, into the huge mysterious forest,
Andredswald, full of deer and boar and strange beasts
And murmuring with small birds, hawks and pheasants.
Soon, with axes and ploughs, they carved out clearings
And made settlements at Fletching and Barcombe,
And some in canoes pressed on to Ardingly.
They built wooden houses and brought up their children,
And fished and took water from the friendly salt free streams.
Later they built many watermills for corn and fulling cloths
They smelted iron as the Celts and Romans had.
Their hammer ponds on the river brought prosperity,
Pouring out the cannon for later centuries' wars.

Walking on the Downs we may dream of the Flecci.
In Norman times did the larks rise and sing for them
As they did for us in the Nineteen-Forties War?
Did immemorial dewponds offer calm and peace
Reflecting dark but passing clouds?
Sheep scribbling on the hills,
Pigs grunting in the yard,
Nights with dazzling stars for light,
Were they hope for the Flecci of return to normal life?

Northward we see no fearful Andredswald
But gentle farmlands of the Weald;
Rape-yellow and viridian and earthy brown;
Red roofs of villages, and gleams of water;
Small stone churches point from knolls of trees
On mounds where once the Flecci built in wood.
And men still fish beside the Ouse
And sail their yachts on reservoirs at Barcombe and Ardingly.

Once a year the people come to the County Show
And celebrate their agricultural heritage.
Should we remember the Flecci then
And the bounty the Ouse has given us?

Irene Wainwright-Snatt

My Most Precious Three

My most precious three are to treasure,
They are unique in their own measure,
Amazing daughter, wonderful mum and lovely man,
All make a difference because they can,
But with bad health, illness and time taking its toll
It makes me worry how things will go,
To love them all no matter what
Makes you realise the love that you've got,
These strong people are so important to me,
They are my world, my most precious three.

My Little Brown Hen

My little chicken is so tame
She is so friendly and knows her name
Clucking contently on the grass
She comes running to me when she's asked
Doris is such a wonderful pet
She's one of the best I've ever met.

Christine Frances Williams

SHEPPERTON

Historic river flows
Enriching meadowland
Where ancient tribes abide,
In simple village harmony
At peace, as farms and orchards thrive
And gently metamorphose
Into our modern age, a land
Where gardens lush
Replace the orchard groves,
The farms receding
Amidst the built-up sprawl
Of houses small or grand
And soon a railway links metropolis,
As shops and restaurants abound
Along a high street brightly graced
With flowerbeds and baskets
Riotous with colours which expand
And complement a spirit of community,
The summer heralds fairs and festivals
In village hall, in churches, schools and parks,
Whilst in November wreaths are laid in memory
Of those whose courage gave us this peaceful land,
Christmas joy invigorates December chill
With carols round an ancient tree,
A sleigh with merry Santa Claus,
A carousel, hot snacks for one and all
And entertainment from a local band,
Local history brings delight
Whilst famous studios produce
Those classic tales and crimes are solved
In quintessential comedy when
Inspector Clouseau shows his hand,
Surely angels alight as birdsong
Wakes us from a wintry dawn,
As spring unfurls in daffodils
Our Shepperton, by Thames, is truly blessed
And gardens bloom on meadowland.

Lorna Troop

Woodland

Sweet scented violet air the woods tranquil
As the orange sun rises over the hill
Upon the top you can see down to the sea
Small fishing boats have returned to the quay
Bustling the fishermen happy; cheerful
Their lobster pots today were full
As the golden sun glints high in the sky
Busy bumblebees black furry gold hum nearby
The nectar sweet, wild the ripe strawberries grow
Butterflies on gossamer silk wings dip low
Ivy clad the inn by the riverside is ancient; old
Its welcome friendly warm, the liqueur pure gold
The sky fiery red as the sun sets behind the hill
Shadows encroach the woodland cools all is tranquil

Sheila Pharo

The Sea Wall

I can see the boats in the harbour
There masts all standing tall
The sun dances on the water
As I walk along the sea wall.
It's so beautiful and still
In the early Sunday morning air
I stop and gaze at the hill
The cows are grazing there.

Underfoot the heavy morning dew
Has soaked my feet to the bone
Mist has rolled in to spoil the view
I think it's time I headed home
The sheep seem to ignore me
Sea wall turns to bridleway
Not long not 'til that cup of tea
And another hazy, lazy day.

Robin Grigsby

Wiltshire

The rolling downs, the cockerel crows,
The wishing wells, the rambling rose.

The thatched cottage roofs
The goose on the farm,
The smell of sweet hay
The swallows in the barn.

The old stone walls
The sheep, the golden corn,
The amber sunsets at early evening
And early dawn.

The streams, the brooks
The woodland's magic charm,
The running of the deer
No threat, no harm.

The horse, the cart
The big oak trees in the park,
The ringing of church bells
Tender moments in your heart
My home, beautiful Wiltshire,
My song like the skylark.

Maddie Reade

Fresh Air

Unspoilt beauty of the Cotswolds
Somewhere special to explore
Sleepy villages full of old charm
Farms where life is tradition
Land to be worked, and stock to care for.

High up in the Downs where kites fly
Children play to their hearts content
Freedom and fresh air to breathe
Nature has its magic wonder.

Joy Milligan

Wish You Were Here – In Swanage

They came from the North to the sea
They thought it the place they should be
Nobody guessed it would rain
The South has the sun just like Spain.
Next morning they went to the beach
The two miles that's called easy reach.
Paid for a deckchair and then sat
wearing mackintosh and a sun hat.
The wind played an eye-stinging game.
Sandwiches lived up to their name.
For three long hours they stayed
then found an amusement arcade.
Lost four pounds in five and ten ps
Bought some post cards of very blue seas.
Six sticks of lurid pink rock
and an ashtray that looked like a clock.
By then it was ten past three
So they went to a café for tea.
They stayed as long as they could.
The weather wasn't looking too good
but Dad said the day was quite warm
so they all ventured out in the storm.
Found shelter in a shop until five
and left hoping they would survive
With a pound and a half of loose sweets
And some foot spray for hot achey feet.
As the rain was now only a shower
They walked around for an hour.
Looked at some boats and some ships,
ate winkles, hot dogs and some chips.
They found a pub that sold mild
With a dart board and room for a child.
So they stayed in there until ten –
And the next day did the same thing again.

Susan Ireland

THE NAZE

(For the teeth collectors)

At sunset the jewel pushes rays through tetchy clouds
Soaking distant rooftops with shrouds
of orange, pinks
Black shadows that reach the seafront
Swimming inwards as the creeping shunt.

The sphagnum of the estuary expands
as if awoken by a termagant
As the throng of gulls flap and peck some singing
Permanent
length of the creeping elbow;
to move our step to some quicker pace.

Nightly they gather above the cliff,
Some communion to feast and praise our distant activity
Searching for mussels, crusts of bread,
Wriggling sand worms that drill in and out
For us to figure on the morning walk,
About what is never seen or said.

From this vantage point, an eye strain across
We come each shorter summer
Pockets full of teeth,
restless
Faces raw with wind and time

And decide on whether to go on;

As the town shadows behind us
The hump of the jewel grows flatter
as a thinning echo,
And the sinking sand reminds us
it would be best for us to return,

Towards the cliff shadow that grows fatter

To beat the tide
That pushes in for the duel.

Stuart Springthorpe

Where I Belong

The wind so wild will steady soon
And clouds that mass to hide the moon
Will break and part and drift away
Impatient with the long delay
Of night with stars that shimmer down
To make for Earth a silver crown
And scented blossom sweet and strong
Will tell me that it's spring e'er long.

The brook will laugh and babble past
The leafy woods with violets cast
And leaping tumbling on her way
Sweep tangled tresses apt to stray
And trail and twine themselves and free
Unruly thatch of willow tree
The thrush will voice his morning song
And day so grey will pass e'er long.

Chimneys smoking black with smuts
Roads with holes and gaping ruts
The air is dank with Winter's woe
A cold grey scene from Summer's foe
And as he breathes his chill raw air
Freezes roost and moor and lair
I long to leave the jostling throng
And walk thro' fields of corn e'er long.

Corn that grows down by the mill
Fanned by the breeze that climbs o'er the hill
Refreshed by the rain that gently falls
Warmed by the sun o'er the old farm walls
Shaded by the boughs of the chestnut tree
Ripening to gold for all to see
Then am I there where I belong
And the world shall be in tune e'er long.

Alma A Sewell

GATWICK

Once the site of racing horse,
Now she reigns a different course
And governs lanes where creatures fly,
Whose open wings dissect the sky.

In past time over Lowfield Heath
The clouds bedecked the sky.
The church is all remains beneath
Them when they're scudding by.

When dawn emerges from the grey,
The sun bestows reluctant ray
Which trips upon the dormant freight
Proclaiming; time will not abate.

A giant quadrille travel mart,
All madding peoples join and part,
Cavorting to their starting gate.
Their empty vessels lay in wait.

Rousing engine starts to whine,
Turning, swirling great turbine,
And when the impetus is more
The woken being starts to roar.

Along the runway lumbers that
Which with the ground should stay intact.
It treads the air: begins to rise
Gatwick Airport rules the skies!

Gillian Lewin

Rural Bliss

Dawn chorus is a joy to hear
But not so many birds now alas.
Reasons various are given for this
But we feed those that do appear.

Honeysuckle suckles the bees
And we grow sunflowers for them too.
We have a stream, ponds and hedges
And flowers bloom with relative ease.

The orchard trees are pruned to scale
They're sprayed for bugs and scab.
They blossom in due time
Produce their fruit for market sale.

Our smallholding involves a lot of work
But it is a way of life
It doesn't produce much profit
But seeing the produce is the perk.

All the seasons have their sway.
The narrow lanes encircle round.
What beauty there is to behold
We thank God as well we may.

So this is our haven place
Time has stood still for us.
Modern world is a short drive away
But we return happily to our base.

Margaret Deverson

My Earthly Home And My Heavenly Home

The lovely county of Hertfordshire – my home for forty years,
Supports the winding River Lea with wildlife, locks and weirs.
Prior to 1850, The Old Pond lived up to its name;
Not a place of beauty – rather a place of shame.
If a husband was displeased, by the actions of his wife,
Publicly she would be ducked – would that end the strife?
The pond's filled up, a fountain marks the centre of Cheshunt today;
And as you pass, if the wind is up, you sometimes feel the spray.
A mile to the north is The Anchor Pub, where sorrows supposedly drown;
It seems to me that they swim well, drink cannot keep them down.
Fifty yards on from the landmark pub, with an anchor for all to see,
Is a little old chapel – by the bus stop it stands – which means such a lot to me.
'The Mission' 'twas called in yesteryear – 'Mill Lane Mission' by some
Beside it is a newer hall, with the same invitation – Come.
See the Lord of Glory, God's most Holy Son,
Hanging on a cross of shame for nothing He had done.
There the wrath of God He bore, the punishment for sin;
In love He suffered, in love He died, that we might be with Him.
Greater love has no man than this, His sufferings disfigured His form;
His face was so marred, His wounds were so deep – that we might be reborn.
Born again into God's family sublime, is God's desire for you;
He is not willing that any should perish, He wants to make us new.
He wants to cleanse us from our sin – the punishment He bore;
Repenting of our sinful ways, there is new life in store.
He will forgive, if we repent, and then we start anew –
Living for Him and not ourselves – seeking His will to do.
God longs to have you as His own – but He does not compel;
He yearns to save each one of us, from the dread horrors of hell.
I've been forgiven, my soul is saved, Christ longs to save you too;
Because God's faithful to His word, I'm gong to Heaven – are you?

For the wages of sin is death; but the gift of God is eternal through Jesus Christ our Lord.
From The Bible, which is God's word to us, Romans 6 verse 23.

Marion Tinkler

Heroes Of My Region In Kent

World War One will be remembered for 'The Battle of The Somme'.
World War Two will be remembered for 'Kent's Biggin Hill Aerodrome.
Where Spitfires and Hurricane's went on missions from this fighter station.
'The Battle of Britain' began, many air crew died, to save our 'Mother Nation'.
I am proud being raised in this part of Kent
Where Thomas Durrant a Victoria Cross soldier and his brother Jack
when boys to the village school went.
It was 'The Raid at St Nazaire' where Sergeant Thomas Durrant
V.C. put Kent on the map, as did his brother Jack
awarded 'The Military Medal', and the local villagers will
never forget that.
Our village Hero Thomas Durrant and his brother Jack
brought much pride as well as tears
So too did the 'Biggin Hill' pilots who in combat showed no fears
World War Two remains local history in this region of Kent
With memories of young men who lost their lives
as off to war they went.
Now their names are etched on memorial plaques each one.
Their young lives they sacrificed for our country
And remembering them forever will live on.
For as long as the sunshine follows the rain
A rainbow will appear in the sky
And these young Heroes will be looking down on Earth
Their spirit will never die.

Brenda Casburn-Colvin

OLD CHATHAM

I'm a Chatham girl
I know Chatham
Oh so very well
I was born here
Lived here
All my life
Became married
Became a wife
I'm a true cabbage islander
Through and through
If I ever left here
What would I do?
Yet I reminisce for the old Chatham
Of long, long ago
Which I want
So badly
To know
If I could turn back
The clock of time
Close my eyes
And be there
In my mind
In that old Chatham Town
Of long ago
With its horses
And carriages
I'd travel around
I'd be in Heaven
My feet wouldn't
Touch the ground
In that old Chatham Town.
I have heard.

Charles Dickens
In his time
Had walked
These great lines
In Old Chatham
Of long ago
The one
I really wish
I could know
That old Chatham Town
That old Chatham
Of so long ago.

Barbara Towes

THE WATERWAY OF KENT

There's a sunlit-dappled welcome
Where the willows weep and sigh
For a youthful Medway's frolicsome intent,
Down through Edenbridge and Chiddingstone,
By Penshurst Place and Leigh,
To be worthy of the title of The Waterway of Kent.

Through the Wealden water meadows,
Past the blossom and the bine;
Out of Tonbridge, on to Maidstone, seaward bent.
Where the voices of the Kentish men
And Men of Kent combine
To extol the River Medway as the waterway of Kent.

Let them sing of bonnie Clyde and
Let them sing of Father Thames;
Let them tell their tales of Tyne and Tees and Trent,
Of the Severn, Wye and Humber
And of lesser watery gems –
We shall answer with: 'The Medway is the waterway of Kent!'

Alan Bignell

The Thames Valley

Spring had turned into summer, winter had long passed by,
Sun rays were beaming down heat from a clear blue sky.
The River Thames runs through an area close to our home,
A walk near its bank we thought, a good place to roam.
With expectations high, we then started our day,
And first glimpse of this river took our breath away.
Although the river gave the impression of might,
What surrounded it made such a wonderful sight.
Wide open spaces across a valley so vast,
Exposing a panorama that only Nature could cast.
As trees in their thousands for miles could be seen,
Some leaves turning gold when once they were green.
Evergreen bushes where their leaves never shed,
Producing many berries, yellow, orange and red.
Hills and dales covered with fields meet the eye,
All blending together to reach the blue of the sky.
Villages and houses dotted around small and frail,
Almost looked as if put there from the Lilliput tale.
As we tried to take in all this beauty around
Three swans flew over, such a percussion of sound.
And kites glided around in the cushions of air,
With fantastic wing spans keeping them there.
We progressed further as the river gently did wend
And our walk took us round a very small bend.
Where large elegant houses from the top rank
Displayed picturesque lawns rolling down to the bank.
The river was now showing perspectives quite new,
As the ripples from boats sparkled like diamonds do.
The swans now swimming after their breathtaking flight
And the sails from many yachts billowing white.
Then near to the bank, weeping willow trees were seen,
Their leaves a mixture of colours, silver and green,
Erect and in line they glistened in the sun's glare,
These willows weren't weeping but brought happiness there.
As we turned for home the swans were now being fed,
Many children were laughing and throwing them bread.
Then a gaggle of geese all in line filled the air,
Another sight to thrill us before leaving there.
Then happy people in boats were waving our way,
Which put a wonderful end to a magical day.

Bill Tapping

The Little Old Lady Of Bromley By Bow

Upstairs on the landing
A large house in London
Sits my little of lady of Bromley by Bow
Looks down every morning
From half-open windows
And sees all the pushing impersonal people
Who pass by her window, but none of them knows
My little old lady
Looks down from her landing
In lost hours of living
In Bromley by Bow.

No doubt she is dreaming
Of someone to hold her
Is my little old lady of Bromley by Bow
A sad smile she's wearing
A warm heart she's sharing
And sends all her suitors bouquets of her sunshine
So sailors may hornpipe and pipers may blow.
My little old lady
Calls out from her window
For someone to talk to in Bromley by Bow

Her hall has a picture
The loves long forgotten
Of my little old lady o Bromley by Bow.
Her scrap book of sunshine
Of children in braces and babies in rompers,
The bromide is fading but memories grow.
My little old lady
Throws sweets from the window
For children to gather in Bromley by Bow.

Her face wears no longer
The worry of waiting
For my little old lady of Bromley by Bow.
New neighbours are showing
Fresh curtains are blowing,
New people are coming, new paint on the doorstep,
A box in her window where daffodils grow.
My little old lady
Now talks to the angels.
God took her to Heaven from Bromley by Bow.

Chris Porteous

A Walk In Forster Country

Walking from the church of Saint Nicholas
Stevenage
Past sleeping 'celebs' in the churchyard by,
Where Cypress trees stand elegantly tall and
Marble headstones shimmer starkly in
bright sunlight.
Huge black ones with gold lettering,
Kneeling angels, and temple mounts
Crosses of all shapes and sizes,
I bowed in prayer to the sleeping dead.

Out onto the road with careful tread
'Keep well into the side,' the leader said.
In single file we paced our steps
On a winding lane with a very high hedge
Past buddleia just about to flower,
I spied peacock and tortoiseshell butterflies
basking in the sunshine.

On to 'Rooks Nest House' Forster's childhood home
Where he played tennis with his friends on the front lawn,
The house feature in his novel 'Howards End' but
In my head I conjured the music of Elizabeth Poston and
Pictured Malcolm Williamson conducting,
Back on to the lane, some tall trees formed a green arch.

Chesfield Park was our next destination
Once home to the Seebohm Quaker family,
The C17 house was cruelly demolished
The present one blends quite beautifully
We walked all around right joyfully
Skirting the estate most carefully.

The afternoon was very hot
We could smell the scent of honeysuckle
In full bloom in the hedgerow,
We tramped over stubbled fields where
Dead trees stood ghostly and stark in the broad daylight,
We caught sight of buzzards circling high
in the bright blue sky.

Reaching the ruins of Chesfield Church
Within the now near vanished village
A gruesome story was recalled,
A dispute over parish boundaries
Between the two vicars
Resulting in one vicar murdering the other.

Resting, we drank water that had warmed in the hot sun
Gazed at leafy patterns of sunlight through the trees,
Sat in awe before the statue of Etheldreda
Contemplated the life of this East Anglian princess
Who married twice but retained her virginity,
Her devotion to God was viewed in perceptivity

Now homeward bound we made our way
Round wide fields full of hay,
Between furrows deep we spied wild orchids, while
In the distance St Nicholas' spire gleamed bright,
As the bells rang out for Evensong
We would be home before long.

Kathy Dickenson

THE REDOUBT

Round and large, it towers above the little town below
A guardian; a sentinel built many years ago.
Built in a time of threatened war to keep the foe away
It stood; its gunports ready to fire across the bay.

Although expensively equipped with weapons great and small,
They never fired in anger, if they ever fired at all.
And so the fortress lay forlorn all through Victorian days
Until in a new century war did its spectre raise.

A prison, then. Its walls held firm 'gainst soldiers who had fled
And later still, used to prepare for the great atomic dread.
Sad and neglected once again; a rubbish dump; o'ergrown
Till dedicated workers came to make its history known.

Now it still stands above the town; restored inside and out.
The union flag still flying o'er the fine Harwich Redoubt.

Frances Russell

My Essex Home

I climb over the gate into the woods
The rabbits scatter away,
A little fawn leaps in the grass
As if he wants to play.

Bluebells and wild garlic
Are swaying in the breeze,
Growing tall in the shadowed light
Underneath the cedar trees.

Seagulls are following the plough
Next to a field of Friesian cows
And a choir of songbirds sing.

Wild roses bloom along the way
On this beautiful summer day
I know that I will always stay
In my home by the sea.

As I look to the sky a buzzard
Glides on wings so high.
The song birds seem to disappear
So quickly now, so full of fear.

I walk along the sandy path
And smell the salty air,
The sea is coming in to sight,
Sea cabbage is growing everywhere.

Red poppies and daisies shine
In the morning dew
And where could I ever wish for a
Nicer view.

Vivian Chrispin

The Valley

You wind your way through Cuxton
Then on up Sundridge Hill
There you'll see a beautiful sight
To agree I know you will.

You can look down through the valley
Each field looks lush and green
And the woods that run along the top
Now look how they once would have been.

Because chalk from the hills was extracted
And from the riverbanks they dug clay
With water they mixed the two together
And burnt it in a special way.

Factories pumped out sulphur
In their bid to make cement
Many employed day and night
And supplying them houses to rent.

Scars on the landscape are now healing
And many factories not seen
Slowly Nature's taking over
Now it's a much cleaner scene.

It's nice to see a factory free valley
But doubt in my inner thoughts lurk
Now we've got a lush green valley
We've got nowhere now to work.

Barry.G.Randall

My Place, My Area To Explore

I live in a village called Kemsley,
With a pub, shop, bowling green and village hall,
Also not far, just round the corner
The surgery, chemist and post office too.
On a main bus route into town.
Also cycle routes and walks to explore
Around the ponds, country parks,
Listen carefully in summer skies, skylarks.
Pick the blackberries in country lanes,
To make your blackberry and apple pie.
But if this does not take your fancy
Catch a train to the shore, it's so near.
The journey will excite, not bore,
Relax on the beach,
Listen to the shingle rolling in off the sea
Ah! That relaxes me.
But fun and excitement can be found
With all sorts of amusements around
When all the fun is done
It's off to McDonald's for a burger in a bun,
When night-time falls, and you go to bed
You'll hear these words,
'Have you had fun?'
'I have,' I said.

David Skinner

The Jewel In The Crown

There's no better place to live than Rye
Buildings tall that reach the sky
The cobbled streets and Mermaid Inn
Where smugglers hid – if they got in.
St Mary's church – with quarter boys loud
And the Landgate Arch makes one so proud
To live in a Cinque Ports town –
The jewel in the crown.

Pat Salisbury-Ridley

My Way

My heart goes out as I see
The countryside confronting me
As I look from left to right
The sea is there, what a sight
Whichever way my eyes do wander
This southern county makes me ponder
All that's beautiful you'll find here
The place to me is so dear
Small villages surround the main
All so lovely, not just plain
Little shops which blow the mind
Tea is served the old-fashioned kind
This heaven is for us to see
God made this for all not just me

Sylvia Ash

Black Park (Iver)

Autumn in Black Park
Is an enchanting place to be
If you like a scenic view
And tranquility.

It is quite fascinating
To see the reds and greens and golds
Of nature's habitat
As winter unfolds

You can relax on a bench
And watch the world go by
And listen to the sound
Of the birds' lullaby.

Or you can watch the sun's reflections
Shimmer on the lake
And make many happy memories
With each photograph you take.

Janet Larkin

AONB

Way down south, in the middle, at the end
A little peninsula rests
Not far enough east to be east
Not far enough west to be west

A farming village surrounded by sea
The quirky incongruity
Of tractors and sails
Egrets and bales
A sort of solid fluidity

Northwards the protective embrace
Of the downs can be seen and felt
And hidden from view the rat race
And some kind of commuter belt
To the east and the west and south
We stick out like a tongue from a mouth
The ocean lapping our sides
Subject to time and tides

And here we can boast
Countryside and coast
To be grounded, yet float
Accessible and remote

Yet our lifeblood, the land, beneath our feet
Solid, safe, secure
The farmers' crops of golden wheat
Where deer and pheasant and seabirds meet
Our roots run, deep and sure

Yet I have seen the ocean's jaws, salty-deep
Reach across and summarily sweep
Root crops from their warm, earthy bed
And suck potatoes back to its stead

A strange beauty we are
So near and yet so far
From the madding crowd
And immensely proud
And protective of this, our place
Like a separate race

No pavements do we boast
We have country paths and coast
'You have no street lights,' strangers say
'Well, we have no streets, so go away'

The moon and stars light our plains
And wiggly, windy country lanes
We have cesspools in our gardens too
So think on before you flush the loo

Before the convenience of the car
Everywhere but where we are
Was 'outside' and not 'us'
Couldn't even get here on a bus
Still can't in actual fact
But cars put paid to that

Now we have been 'found'
And outsiders come around
Somewhere inappropriate they abandon their cars
To tramp our country lanes and paths
With their special boots and sticks and hiking gear
And yet we've not a mountain or hill to show
Ramblers, don't you know!

Then they sample the local and its bitter
Go home and leave us all their litter
It's such a shame, though I'm told, not a sin
That now we can get out, they can also get in

Not so many 'olduns' left now
That used to reminisce of how
The ocean left its very shore
And knocked upon the church's door
Ah! The sea, the sea, you forget it's there, and yet
Deeply felt, the presence of its threat

So, exactly where is this A O N B?
That is land and also sea
Where sailors sail and farmers farm
That is both coast and country charm

Like I said, far south, in the middle, at the end
And that is all you'll get my friend.

Lynda Hughes

Royal Berkshire

Leafy lanes and Berkshire Downs
Title houses and workman's cottages
Windsor Castle and fine royal horses
We 'Salute' you 'Mam' for 60 years on the throne
Never – never to hear you moan
Winning streaks at Ascot races
Thundering past the winning post
Pubs and clubs offering you delicious traditional 'Sunday roasts'
Winding river at its best
Old Father Thames
Soothing place to rest one's head
Fun parks as Legoland to explore
Leaving the kids wanting more
Posh gardens for us slow and elderly
Like Mapledurham House who knows the score
Holds the spirits of the 'Roses' war
Remembering the soldiers' 'bloody fight' for Cromwell's law
Mill wheel turns to grind the corn
Enjoying picnics on the lawn
On the riverbank it does slumber – can you ask for anything more?
There it sits in Reading's Town
The Old Abbey ruins now renowned
Torn and ravaged by King Henry's rage
To release Old England's Soul from Rome's Eternal Cage
Countryside you may travel
Delights one – who stops and stares
At each and every village
Nestling in their lairs
Soft hillsides too will bring you near
To the sweet bubbling sound of the Kennet Canal
Travelling barges takes its flow
Bringing happiness
As they go
Under bridges old and low
Opening each lock – now with no tow
Standing proud upon the hill

Highclere Castle built long ago
With lavish surroundings to hold – Now – Award winning TV show
Or a posh wedding or two
That's if you can afford it – though!
Reading is also famous you know
For starlets like Kate Winslet and film director Kenneth Branagh
And not to forget Ricky Gervais from the hilarious
Again – Award Winning 'The Office' show
Yes! Berkshire born and bred am I
I can hear you sigh
With a tear in my eye
I do – I do – quite happily reside.

Thelma Glanville

A Southend Hospital Ward

A green plant beyond
a window, is buffeted
by wild weather.
A solace to someone,
wracked with pain.
In they come,
young and old,
confused and afraid,
perhaps after a fall.
Nurses rush forth,
to tenderly place them in bed.
This is a female ward,
in our own hospital.
Nurses flit to other wards,
so many who need compassion.
Daughters visit, and weep for Mum.
Men enfold their precious ones.
Families gather around the beds,
and patients' eyes shine
Amidst this circle of love,
he above joins the throng.
Specialists, doctors and nurses
And the son of god
Restore the body and soul,
of everyone in need.

Joan Skinner

Thirty Minutes From London

Thirty minutes from London
Two minutes from the countryside
Seconds away from my garden
Where in peace I can hide

Commerce and industry
Retail and leisure
Centralized within
The bounds of the new town
While all around
Countryside surrounds

Freedom is choice
Choice is freedom
Urban or countryside?

Within minutes
I could be shopping in a busy mall
Or strolling through a leafy wood
I may be on my way to work
Or meandering beside the stream
Rushing from place to place
Or taking time out just to dream

Only thirty minutes from London
If one takes the fast train
Or minutes away from the peace and quiet
Of a leafy country lane

When I first moved to Stevenage
My friends said that I must be mad
And that a concrete jungle
Was no place for a country lad

Yet here I have more access
To the countryside or town
As the south coast is swallowed
By one huge condominium
And what's more besides
We're only thirty minutes from London.

Grant Meaby

Hackney

It's a familiar place with an overcast face
Masked with disgrace
An old pearly queen lace
On the new multicultural race

Steeped in echoes from the past
Ghost grey buildings that survived the blast
As the clock tower bell chimes the hour
The hoards of gangs claim their power

From the haunted graveyard a whisper of Knights with a Templar story
A shiver from the ancestors makes the place gory
A siren in the background, pigeons in the air
The skyline of towering blocks that we share

Pie and mash with jellied eels
Fish and chips to warm the chills
The workman's café for quick-time meals
The re-opened lido in London Fields

Big red buses crammed with people going by
Devil in the corner; getting high

Cockney slang
The choir sang
The gun goes *bang*

Graffiti art on the street
Olympic Games on its feet
Memories of the bullring with the milk crate slide
Behind all the fences the councilors hide

Well Street Market and Vicky Park
Nice in the day but not after dark
The mass of estates; the poverty equates
A problem that pre-dates all of our fates

But under the mask of cool, urban attire
Burns an energy stronger than fire
Because we all love the Hackney Empire.

Sarah Robertson

A Kentish Way

Eastward, the Bromley train
Points toward country of verdant beauty,
Smoothly speeding its comfortable way
Through open Wealden land so green.
Has a better land ever been?

Kentish folk dwell western side
Of the Medway and its flow.
Through their land our route will go
Heading for the North Sea coast
To lands known for *people of Kent*.

Quaintly divided but still united
This county of green orchards,
Fields and marsh for sheep to graze,
Trees a-plenty line curvaceous bounds
Of flowing hill contours that still astound.

Via Rochester, with castle tower,
Cathedral lofty, but not aloof,
What ancient peoples gathered here
Land-hungry Saxons, Danes, and Normans,
All seeking for an enforced share.

Farming villages still abound,
Alongside fast train route to the Continent,
Like Frindsbury of my family fame.
But Great-grandfather, Jesse Giles, farmer's man,
Found and wed Lizzie Wood of Islington.

'tis said a man must have his mate
Shortage of work also his fate.
To leave behind crops and Kent hops brew,
Whitstable oysters, Cox's pippins, too.
Hard was the city's graft he found.

Up long Strood Hill, towards the west,
To seek that wife was his lonely quest.
Unlike those who now seek the sea
And journey on holiday, eastwardly,
He trudged that other direction's way.

A labourer in *the Smoke* was he
East London his new home to be.
Tho' father, Joseph, and wife Jane Hinge,
Stayed settled where they'd always been
'midst downs and fields of Eastern Kent.

For love of Lizzie, babes on the way,
Jesse in smoggy London clime survived.
They grew as part of the city's swelling,
In some cramped and dowdy dwelling.
No regret he e'er came that way?

We can now trace by train or car
The county of Kent of our forebears
Who scraped a living from the soil
But in London also came to toil
By another Way, but ne'er returned.

Jo Allen

The Churchyard Seat View

From the churchyard seat there was lots to see
Such a wonderful view there was before me
There were lots of rabbits all running around
Birds were flying, some singing out loud
The sky was grey, many trees were bare
Deer were grazing everywhere
Roses shone yellow, pink, red and white
Giving light to a grey day, such a beautiful sight
The grass was still green with bare patches too
What a wonderful view I was seeing, it's true
The church in its splendour behind me looked out
On the glorious view I am writing about
I gave thanks to the Lord for the wonderful view
For all His creations I'd seen old and new
Such a blessing to me this time had been
Admiring the creations of God's that I'd seen
Many people come from miles around
To this wonderful place they too have found
Where they find peace and comfort too
On the churchyard seat with a wonderful view
From the churchyard seat on which I sat
God blessed me with this poem and I thanked Him for that.

Royston Davies

Evenings At Ten, Bromley, Kent

Saturdays are fun at Mrs D's place,
Her get-togethers are legendary,
She dominates you with positive grace.

Her piano playing is really ace,
She's loved by every Tom, Dick and Harry,
Saturdays are fun at Mrs D's place.

Bring a song, or some jokes to set the pace,
You have to perform, it's customary,
She dominates you with positive grace.

Not everyone sings, so if you replace,
Well read poetry is necessary,
Saturdays are fun at Mrs D's place.

Get there early, there's not a lot of space,
But creature comforts are secondary,
She dominates you with positive grace.

So pop along, four Jubilee Terrace,
With as many drinks as you can carry.
Saturdays are fun at Mrs D's place,
She dominates you with positive grace.

Alan Dee

My Countryside

My countryside is beautiful how proud am I that I can see
these things around us and they are free.
At this time of year, June, the trees are resplendent
homes for he birds and all their descendants.
I hear the birds singing as they build their nests
this life without them I could never express.
The rabbits go quick to the burrows and hide,
down the lane go the horses side by side.
Large clumps of bluebells carpet the woods,
the small little bells look just like hoods.
I've touched upon a very few things
that this world of ours offers and the pleasure it brings.
Evolution is stirring in my mind
I guess I'm just a special kind.

Patricia Murray

Thoughts On A Postcard

Somewhere amongst my old letters and bills
Is a postcard, black and white,
Of a train approaching Barcombe Mills:
A class 4 tank engine and two coaches
In fading winter light.
You can almost feel the chill.
A lone man in a raincoat waits,
And time stands still.

When I lived in Uckfield I used that line:
From Lewes it crossed low fields beside the Ouse,
Fields glowing in evening sunshine
Or flat gray under shadowed clouds
Which tempered the landscape's lemon hues.
Once, flooded, the fields became a white expanse
Split by the chord of the raised track,
Like a tightrope on which the train could balance.

At Uckfield, dusk, and George the porter took
The tickets; one paused to hear
The departing engine's thunder; then to look
At the red oil lamp
Winking on the receding rear
Coach; George vanished; gas mantles glowed like limelight,
And traffic roared over the level-crossing
As dusk became night.

That old route, like others, ran
To Sussex villages and towns;
Places where now and then one can
Still hear an accent like ripe apples –
As Sussex as the Downs.
Some lines have been revived (in part) by volunteers,
And sometimes far-off whistles may be heard,
Like ghosts of former years.

Michael Irish

Sunset

S un divined atmosphere
U nique rays of vibrant colour
N umerous effect and feelings
S oft delicate rays intense you
E arthly essence of a beautiful day
T iredness drifts away as you and sunset become one.

Unbreen Shabnum Aziz

My Essex

When I say I'm from Essex, people just smile
I'm not born of Essex, but I've lived here a while.

It has so much to offer, and so much to see,
It's all there for the taking, it's all there for free.

Clacton is great, that's why they flock here,
For the sun, sea and air, and Clacton pier.

Walton-on-the-Naze with its famous tower,
You'll want to spend many a happy hour.

There's Mersea Island, unique in its own way,
cut off from the mainland at times of the day.

There's all old Victorian yacht, been there since
Queen Victoria once gave it to a prince.

The oldest recorded town is Colchester, a vital link with our British Army.
If you miss the museum and wonderful castle, I would think you've all gone barmy.

And then there's 'Soufend' as the Londoners would say
A favourite venue in every way.

With its great long pier and a train to ride
No wonder the locals are filled with pride.

We have so much lovely countryside, and so much to see,
I know now why you are smiling, you are jealous of me.

Gordon Miles

Time Will Run Back, And Fetch The Age Of Gold

(John Milton)

A keen, cold, blustery Sunday, set us a task,
because a previous fearful tide had receded
and torn waves apart, ripping off the chalk-cliffs' mask,
now archaeologists were needed

to measure, draw, photograph and excavate bits
the invading sea had for centuries hidden:
traces of ancient dwellings, post-holes; storage pits
(wattle-lined) and nearby, a midden.

Racing against time and clockwork's returning tide,
ignoring ice-dried feet and fingers but not the urge
to find, record more which the mud-holes had to hide,
like a bronze hoard, wrapped in the bark of birch.

Winds, sharp like trowels, revealed outlines of a canoe,
swamped now by swelling waves, cresting our own pain.
we had to beat a hasty retreat, for we knew
this site would not reappear again.*

*Isle of Thanet, Kent.

Jane McCarthy

Rural Kent

The hills of Kent stand clear against the sky
And cloud formations wax and wane as they pass by,
Casting shadows across the expanse of land.
Moving changing patterns controlled by mighty hand!
Oh the wonder, to gaze upon a scene
Of rural splendour; a peaceful summer dream!
With distant humming of 'combine' in the corn,
And rabbits playing, white powder puffs adorned.
Late summer beauty, giving joys that live forever
Within the longing heart tested beyond measure!
God alone could plan such detail in His own perfect way,
Delight to give, to bless, and refresh the soul to meet another day!

Elizabeth Bruce

OUR TOWN

This is our town – a place we know so well,
Those who live here have many stories to tell
Of the pier and the fire that happened one night,
Then the hurricane that hit us before it was light.
Tales of the Kursal and bygone days of glory,
The sea and beach – there's no end to the story.
There are fountains where children love to play
And the Rossi's ice cream the delight of the day.

The people who live here are a mixture of types
They sail in their boats, and fly their own kites,
Some live in big houses, some in small flats
And some have large dogs, and some small cats.
So what do we offer, here in Southend-on-Sea?
Beaches, golf, sailing, the sea – which is free!
There's cinemas, bowling alleys, a train on the pier,
So much to offer – don't you wish you were here?

Although our town is attractive to many folks around,
There are still the same problems here to be found.
The homeless seeking shelter for the night,
The vagrant wandering through the streets so bright.
The family finding the going tough,
The lonely who feel they've had enough.
We are here with them, let's not leave them there.
Be a helping hand to them, show them we care.

So as we live together in this place we love so well
Let's be the friend and neighbour so that others can tell
That this town we live in is a place we want to be
With all the opportunities it offers you and me.
Let's not take for granted all the blessings we have here
The beautiful sunsets we see throughout the year.
The turning of the tides, the seagull's noisy call,
Let us be grateful for these blessings given to us all.

Pauline Hamilton

Gems Of The Thames Valley

In the pretty village of Sonning we never tire
With the lovely lock, the church with its spire.
Look whilst we cross the bridge the Thames does invite,
Into the county of Oxfordshire, what an enchanting sight.
The river here with its wondrous view
Where is anything better? I haven't a clue!
In summer many boats ply their elegant way
Father Thames begs us to stay.
Why not? One asks – let us stop whilst our thoughts give time to reflect
The ambiance of the scene our mind at rest in effect.
Let us pass the college on the river at Shiplake
To the delightful village we make.
How can we deny ourselves the beauty to see
To think this the Thames Valley view is free.
So the pleasant town of Henley gets nearer and almost in sight
A gift we take as our right.
But before then we pass Marsh Lock with the weir
Its gushing water so relaxing and clear.
At Henley the royal county of Berkshire beckons us to come
Onto the delightful stone bridge, a stunning sight to some.
Or you may wish to cross the river some other way
So why not take the short rail journey, a pleasant interlude to make your day.
A few miles to arrive by train at Wargrave gives a different aspect of village life
Complete relaxation from every-day strife.
Then onwards the river and meadows invite
Animals and much birdlife is a wonderful sight.
So onwards we make our way as the day draws to a close
Can one recall a more inspiring walk – who knows?

Peter Parbery

BENEATH OUR FEET

Only the ruins remain, laughing in the sun,
Where the soldiers marched coming from London,
They left the name we know as St Albans,
Were proud tall warriors – they were Romans;
Now I live in their camp and see the legions,
The legacies are here in all our regions,
We imagine rich pickings below our ground,
Pots, coins and daggers have all been found,
We sit by the lake and look towards the arch,
Entrance to the walled city, where conquerors march,
It was over, time to leave England's shores,
The city you occupied is no longer yours,
But without Roman history, it would not be complete,
There's still more to find beneath our feet.

Terry Reeves

THE GARDEN OF ENGLAND

Where are the gardens of England? Aye!
Where are they? Not where the Medway runs
Out to sea past the long silenced guns
Of Dicken's ancient towns where ships lie
Still in the museum shipyard, no! Not there!

Along the shaded vale I search,
Among the chestnut, oak, beech and limes.
Along leafy lanes, 'mid bowers of birch.
Few are the orchards of former times.
Those that remain are bankrupt, bare

The hop vines flower no more, beer still flows,
Allotments and home gardens flourish
And many display at the annual shows.
More and more compost their rubbish.
Yet the Garden of England, where oh! Where?

John Stanbridge

LEIGH OLD TOWN

The town is small, it's on the coast, small houses hug the shore,
When sun is shining folks flood in, do they know what went before?
Before the trains cut through its heart and tore its buildings down,
Took homes away, made people leave and left us half a town.
The cockle boats still ply their trade, fresh seafood always there,
Folks eat the catch and drink the beer, are none of them aware?
We are steeped in history, the Mayflower moored here,
It gathered Leigh people, America bound, with many a sorry tear.
Just by the benches where people sit and watch the sun go down
Are the old stone steps John Wesley climbed when he landed in the town.
He built his first small chapel here, it still stands today
Is it still used I wonder, do folks still come to pray?
In World War Two our little boats to Dunkirk bravely went,
Saved many of our stranded lads and Leigh lives were sadly spent.
We have many festivals, folks flood our streets and play
Do any of them know or care what went on before today?

Lesley Gill

ESSEX PIECE OF WOODLAND
(In dedication to Martin Lawrence Miller)

Dear love of mine, he was so beautiful,
as were these flower-strewn woods he loved before
he ever gave himself to Death. Then sore,
the darkest tempest raged by Nature's law;
now trunks high-heaped upon the leafy floor
are rotting, victims of the fungus spoor –
and yet these too are very beautiful.
May God forbid a desecration's line
of housing, or a concrete snake entwine
the sodden ground, which now is yours and mine!
How did you know, how dared you so define
that Nature's private woods, without a trace,
could cause the death, in her own lonely space,
of those intruders in her secret place?
Yet too these rotting woods are beautiful.

Janet Miller

Sussex Is Home To Me

Cloud shadows drift across the South Downs
White cliffs 'Seven Sisters' gleam in the sun
Beyond is a glimpse of summer blue sea.
Sussex is home to me.

Horsham tiled cottages round village greens
Little grey churches – portrait brasses to see
Stories of witches and good pharisees.
Sussex is home to me.

Arundel Castle stands strong through the ages
St Richard's Cathedral with sky reaching spire
Fragments of Roman villas discovered.
Sussex is home to me.

Family holidays – long remembered,
   buckets and spades on golden sands.
Seaside Towns with warmest welcomes
A crab sandwich for lunch – strawberry ice creams!
Sussex is home to me.

Brighton's Lanes for antique seekers
Historic houses and gardens to view
Country walks with wild flower meadows.
Sussex is home to me, now.

Meryl

Bluebells

It was through woodlands, I wandered as in a trance,
When suddenly, oh, such wondrous view – by chance
I came upon 10,000 bluebells, as far as could be seen
Colours, mixing together, azure, cobalt and ultramarine.

In spring bluebells paint the woodlands with delight
While romanticizing with the natural landscape sight.
There their heads on tall stalks appearing to dance
As they swayed in the breeze, and seemed as if to sing.

'Admire our short beauty, while you may
for we are a sign of the welcoming in of the spring.'

Irene Briscoe

The Beautiful Countryside

The grass seems so much greener,
On the other side of the fence,
The fields a mass of colour,
In shades of yellow so intense,
They light up the horizon,
Then fade out to meet the sky,
In a sea of floating calmness,
With the red kites soaring by.

It's as pretty as a picture,
This scene that meets the eye,
Full of natural tranquility,
Which money cannot buy;
A peaceful view of nature,
To captivate the heart,
And blow away the cobwebs,
From any corners dark.

The birds are all a-twitter,
As sound carries in the breeze,
Chirping comes from up above,
A nest built in the trees,
Fragile bits of this and that,
Woven in a round,
That teeters resting on a branch,
Away from cats on ground.

It's a privilege to witness,
All the countryside I see,
Spreading out for miles around me,
In its beauty which is free.

Marcy Wilcox

LEISURE

Farmers fields, open spaces,
Spreading out to far-reaching places,
Lots of green for you to see,
Birds above all flying free,
Travelling on, on a good day,
Helping people find their way,
Shops, museums, theatre places to see,
All there for you, entrance a small fee,
Try the putting green only ten holes,
But don't forget to take out the poles,
The children's park is always busy,
Swings and roundabouts make you dizzy,
People moving, time to go home,
Tide coming in covering beaches of stone,
Restaurants, pubs, hotels for food and rest,
Down here, south, we sell the best,
When day is over and you plan another day,
Here's hoping you find the second one as good as you did today.

Jean Smith

HORNCHURCH CRICKET CLUB

The sight-screens scroll like camera shutters
Back and forth across the lawn
Capturing creases where square-cutters
Once divided fields of corn.

Strange to think as a spinner wrangles
His wrong 'un towards the blade.
Dick Turpin was still rustling bangles
When cricket here was first played.

Beneath the bough, at the bowlers' end
(The one where the pints are poured)
Sated you'll find us suburban men:
Alas, Lords we can't afford.

To Havering, then, all praise is due
For three centuries of fun.
Allowing flannelled fools to pursue
Across its lush meadows: runs!

Bernard Doogan

Worthing

'Come to sunny Worthing'
The posters on display,
Show a pretty maid with golden locks,
Who will charm your blues away.

But is it always sunny?
Not possible I fear,
But we have the usual attractions,
Like the bandstand and the pier.

You can stroll along the prom, prom, prom,
Or swim in the waters blue,
Walk on the sands, dip your toes in the sea,
And you could come bowling too!

But don't come when it's windy in Worthing,
You might get blown into the sea.
Hold on to your hats and umbrellas,
And make sure you cover your knees!

As seagulls hover and get caught in the slip stream,
And surfers are jumping high,
Skateboarders race with the wind behind them,
And kites go flying high.

I've heard folk come to Worthing
To die, then forget to, they say,
Most people, I know come for just a short while
And never want to go away!

Vera Brown

Remembering Ascot Races In The 1940s

I lay upon the old mile course, dreaming,
Of childhood days, king, queens and horse, streaming,
In gay procession past watching crowd, cheering,
With waving hands and faces proud, peering,
At family royal and coaches run, gleaming.
Under floating clouds and summer sun,
Seeming, seeming, seeming.

Peter Rowe

Waltham Abbey An Old Market Town (In Essex)

Magnificent oak and willow trees
Edge the River Lea
Offering shady walks, sun filtering through the leaves
Creating diamond glints on water rippling in the breeze.

At the water's edge wildlife rear their young
Ducks, swans, moorhens, coots and geese, so graceful every one,
The grass snake across the river glides
Beneath the water's surface, the large pike hides.

Beautiful meadows abundant with flowers
Buttercups, clover, daisies and poppies keep bumblebees busy for hours
The bird of prey hovers beneath the sky
The quarry in the meadow grass, held in the hawk's eyes.

An old stone bridge, the abbey forge,
The orchard surrounded by ancient walls
A fragrant rose garden, an ancient well
The chiming of the old church bell.

The church so beautiful beckons you in
With its huge stone pillars and wonderful carvings
Its stained glass windows and amazing ceiling
Such beauty steeped in ancient history.

The churchyard with friends and loved ones, from this life now gone
Somewhere tranquil for memories to linger on
Benches beneath aged trees
Loved ones rest awhile recalling happy memories.

The old water trough, buildings with gargoyles, the old market place,
Quaint pubs and tea shops
'Sun street' where a warm welcome awaits
Historic Waltham Abbey'
Reputedly, King Harold's burial place.

Sandra Gorton

Provincials

Sit in burnt out pubs and rust.
They slosh their beer, chew their tongues,
wince through smoke, grind another fag-
end into a heaving ashtray. Provincials grit
their teeth and drive fists into bleary eyes
under shadows of ever more timeless days.

You've seen them, sure you know the type:
the blotchy face, the vacant gaze, prison
tattoos of crucifixes and lovers' names
on raw and hairy knuckles. We've seen them
clutching receipts, gobbing on the street,
shuffling home at closing time

to decaying flats above the sky, to the life
we'll never hear about: the daughters
bought expensive gifts and scorned,
the mothers fed and clothed and left alone.
While bohemians snore, provincials sprawl
in unseen rooms and pray.

Brendan Whitmarsh

Kingley Vale

Resonant with age,
boughs long since bowed
upon familiar ground,
humming the drones
of a thousand years.
In the vale of the kings
never gone,
lie upon
the land of fruit and yew.
Glorious strategy
with a glorious view.

Paul Schofield

Sheerness Streets O'my

Dawn about the town house
walking fleet on the street
Fluffs of gaily printed litter
flutter about my feet
Alone in a haze of sunlight
a hose of water down
Gritty pavement gutters
align this road into town.

Tall gaunt shad'ed bowers
crispin windowpanes
Printed painted sigh-written signboards
façade deluged streets fill by rain
Over and down the Broadway
maligned by tulips and a lawn-feed grass
To know your where of whereabouts
all one needs do is ask
Where once a shaded walkway
a cinema for the stars
Now a shop for ice cream, pop, ices
and a host of chocolate iced milk bars.
The boy brings in the display boards
the proprietor brings down the blind shades
the shutters close on the display shelf
another's day is made.
and so the clock hands reach the five hour
half-past four of five they close
to buy and sell means, money, power
Who drives the clock's hands do you suppose?
No, it isn't me, it isn't you,
no not thee or I
here I close my writing down
My poem ends on the Sheerness streets, O'my

Robert John Collins

The Secret Brook

Set below the parkland grass
Hidden by hawthorn and willow fast
The bank tall and rugged
All is peaceful and quiet
As minnows and tiddlers swim along by it
Shallow clear water identifies the brook
Pebbles you will see if you take a look
A sandy bed hides stones and shells
Whilst round about the little vole dwells
The frog, the toad, the stoat and weasel
Kingfisher, heron, the wren and the mistle (thrush)

Silent and still, tranquil and calm
Children love to fish by the brook
Safe from harm
To hear the birds twitter
To see the fish bite
To feel the soft sunrays
Pushing through, bringing light
What a wonderful feeling
What a wonderful day
The brook is pure heaven
A great place to play

Bring your wellies, your rod and your bucket
Bring your friend and with any luck
It will be a good day with the fish biting well
Bring your picnic, your comics as well
It is holiday time, we are free to roam
It is holiday time, let's enjoy the foam
It is holiday time, let's have lots of fun

The silent brook shallow and still
Ripples and twinkles below the hill
Vacant and empty, steady and slow
Wrapped in warm greenery, where?
No one knows!

Answer:
Plumpton Green/E Sussex

Margaret Bennett

Historic Dunstable

Travel down that old Roman road
Where many feet have often strode,
That wondrous, wondrous, Watling Street,
The route to Dunstable is quite elite.
It was once one of the old coaching towns,
Now much more famous for its zoo and downs,
Whipsnade Zoo as its much better know,
And cut into the hillside, a white lion is shown.
On Dunstable Downs they go riding, or gliding,
When rolling the orange, poor children are sliding,
If you should come here and travel around,
The places of interest just simply about.
There's Mead open farm with its sheepdog display,
With mini golf and tractors for children to play.
The Cross Keys is a pub of a good age,
Still situated in Tottenhoe Village
And keep traveling out on the road to Aylesbury,
Still standing, a wonderful windmill to see.
In Church Street a wonderful church stands with pride
Where once Thomas Dun was said to ride
On a black fiery horse, our highwayman did perch,
As he rode past the grounds of the priory church.
In the main street itself, are a few artifacts,
Like the old sugar loaf, for folk to relax.
Part of the old town hall still remains,
From the time Dunstable had horses and reins.
With a little theatre that holds but a few,
But then always willing to try something new.
Surrounded by country, and fields on all sides
A fabulous place where our family resides.

John Bright

Historic Runnymede

In 1215 King John he sealed
The Magna Carta at Runnymede field.
A bold and original step was made
And parliament's powers were summarily laid.

The 'Mother of Parliaments', England became;
No more would royalty call the game.
The common man a vote would hold
No longer for ever to be told.

Through decades and centuries evolved our life,
We battled on through the worst of strife
With parliament and royalty hand-in-hand,
Working always to protect our land.

Today we live in a global age
Where other countries' problems outrage
Our own society, evolved from strife
To a democracy mapping our daily life.

Margaret Gane

My County

Sussex is my county, it's been very kind to me
The countryside is so beautiful and it's easy to reach the sea.
Burgess Hill is where I live, a busy little town
Was known for making bricks from the clay in the ground.
Ditchling Beacon is not far from me
This beautiful spot is for all to see.
Way up high with the birds and bees
Worries forgotten, all at ease.
A panoramic view from the top
Down below towns, villages and shops
Up here sheep grazing on the land
Riders on horseback waving a hand.
Sussex is in my heart, it is in my veins
She is everything that she claims
I love her rivers, I love the sea
I give thanks for all she's given me.

Gladys C'Ailceta

O Pantiles We Rejoice In Thee

The fairest heart of Tunbridge Wells
Beats for me from centuries past,
A voice that speaks and sweetly tells
Of ancient legends that will forever last.

O Pantiles we rejoice in thee
In your warming tiles 'neath our shifting feet,
To catch the blackbird's song in every blooming tree
A bright, sweet place where lovers meet.

We may view down yonder Alley Pink
Unto the shadows where the Coach & Horses Pass,
By the Duke's Tavern where sojourners drink
Of every ilk, satin and silk and the ragged class.

The maid at the springs dips from crystal wells
Magical water cures ague and dull distemper,
And the word soon spreads o'er hills and dells
The Glorious Pantiles they'll always remember.

O Pantiles we rejoice in thee, so finely made
Thy timbered dwellings and gaming rooms,
Lords and Ladies parade in a honeysuckle Colonnade
Where song and laughter and happiness blooms.

O Pantiles we rejoice in thee.

Brian Gamage

Summertime In Bedfordshire

From the Downs five counties can be seen,
Little thatch cottages and old churches going back in time,
Village greens, country lanes, meadows and fields of golden corn,
Butterflies and bumblebees, wild flowers blowing in the breeze.
Horses trotting, walkers ambling through pastures,
And the trees enjoying summertime by rivers and the streams.
Take a walk in Bedfordshire and see the countryside
In all its shades of green.

Yvonne Golledge

A Moving Sonnet

Dream on about the coast and living there
Where London's fumes and grime shall never taint.
Escape and dwell and breathe such pleasant air
Where poets are inspired and painters paint.
Where time seems slower paced and all is quaint.
'Hark, dream no more, for I have heard your plea'
– So spake the fervent dreamer's patron saint –
'I have a place called Bexhill on the sea,
And herein lies your dreamed tranquility.'

So move you urban dweller; wrench away
And salvage basic things; like sanity.
Then breathe again and live another day.

Dislodge me from this rut, this life etched groove
Uproot my stubborn soul; to seaward move.

Leslie Dennis Pearce

Hastings Pier 1980

The misty, blue spring day
Embraces a moving grey sea
Which rushing shoreward hungrily nibbles
At cliffs of brick and stone.

On this straining peninsular
Of wood and rust-freckled iron
People move to and fro,
Visitors from another time and place
Who for a moment fill up
Echoing and vibrant spaces.
The clamour of the fun arcade
Is drowned in gentle conversation
While anglers cast hopeful lines
And watch the gulls brush the sky
With familiar white wings.

Anthony Green

A Specimen Dahlia

I live in a truly brilliant and unique place
Stones throw away from life's great race . . .
Our wildflower garden is my favourite place,
I can lose myself from life's great race . . .
And across my road, the bank of our stream
Our pretty wild garden, really is a dream . . .
A village with shops, Fox Pub and Indigo Café,
And the church by the green where children play . . .
The six-thirty club meet, for those who live alone,
Takes people out, coffee and cake, away from home . . .
Just a mile away, Farnham Town, place of history,
Bishops from London to Winchester, over Hogs Back, name a mystery.
Staying at the castle, carriage through the huge gate,
Town's architecture of Georgian buildings, our region is great . . .
Gostrey Meadow, bandstand, live music, children skipping around,
Knitted scarf in red, white and blue for Jubilee, a real diamond
The Maltings, where children go fishing in the River Wey
A duck race and paddling feet, is really OK . . .
I won the allotment's cup for the best specimen dahlia,
Held at the Maltings, the mayor in full regalia . . .
Leisure centre, museum, art galleries and a university,
Why not come and visit, there is much to see . . .
Where I live, is special, so what can I say,
Our community of lovely people hip hip hooray . . .
And in this busy world, I can feel so carefree,
I am a worldwide published poet of Stream Valley.

Jenny Williams

HOME

This place in which I live
Generously seems to give
The hills with their varied climbs
The parks picnics with cooling wines
The ever-changing coastal shore
Who on Earth could ask for more.

The multi-racial colour skin,
This place I love to live in
The desert dunes and icy glades
Presidential, king and queens parades
The creatures great and very small
OMG I love them all.

Historic streets of days gone by
With new builds to catch the eye
A shanty town with roofs of tin
Or mud huts that the tribes live in
A tall glass tower for money men
My secret place I call my den.

With sparkling stars we share at night
The changing moon to put things right
Where I go and all I see
And what it's really worth to me
My fellow man from place of birth
I love my home, this planet Earth.

C. D. Spooner

LONDON IN NOVEMBER

Daybreak,
The velvet black turns indigo;
Background traffic hum screams out eternally.
The dawn brings deafening roars of arriving jets in scores,
Heathrow's din;
East, riven.
Sky deal flown passengers, like lost sheep, are suddenly absorbed,
Into an impasse, enclave, the holiday best be forgotten;
In the passport nightmare's,
Vocal war.

Awake,
To well kept flat in Pimlico;
Flat-bound Catherine Nunn dreams of maternity.
Performing menial chores, watch her writhe at venial flaws,
Ego's sin;
Priest-shriven.
Ideal Homes lounges, the cost's cheap, are instantly transformed,
Into an Aladdin's cave of polyester and cotton;
After fast shop at Fine Fare's,
Local store.

King's Cross,
North wind blows, makes my eyeballs sting;
Hoodies outside station, spray paint walls illegally.
Floribunda flowers, all wilt and die in bowers,
Faded blooms;
Poor tea rose.
Wafted sweet fragrance, made the sky full, like bread mixed with leaven,
Attacking the blight of blindly ignoring,
That God's cohesive power,
Spins the Earth.

Stained glass,
Torch windows, wakes a high calling;
Goodies tout salvation, at grey St Paul's Cathedral spree.
Torrid thunderclouds, will fill the sky like shrouds,
Day of doom;
War heroes.
Oxford Street vagrant reads the Bible, his head fixed in Heaven,
The black ink on white, solemnly gives a warning,
That there is no peace without the
Pains of birth.

Media,
Tradition breeds a national pride;
Religious rituals at blessed Cenotaph.
Steps with history hewn, with blood-red poppies strewn,
Troops bleed on;
Fields in south.
Bustling worlds of noise, I turn off the main street to the galleries,
There David Hockney's paintings are a pep pill;
In hazy sun, wealth-cliques scan azure
Swimming pools.

Greedier,
A pigeon feeds, irrational-eyed;
Delicious victuals, his chest feathers puffed.
Pecks at the stale crumbs, from office party churns,
Dudes feed on;
Meal fills mouth.
Hustling girls and boys, burn off, with pained feet, the calories,
Where avid Cockneys sprint upon the treadmill,
Gymnasium health-freaks can assure,
'Slimming's cool!'

Policeman,
His finger on the taser gun;
Thinks how he is stressed, longs to escape, so wistfully,
At quarter to five, the shiny, glowing vehicles drive,
Weave in lanes;
Pall Mall squeals.
The cab driver jokes with ease and mirth, sardonically,
Rustic men climb out, two proceeding to busk;
Singing 'Stairway to Heaven',
Daylight palls.

Cerise sun,
Lingering long, the laser sun;
Sinks now in the west, orange sky-scape glows blissfully.
Near Waterloo's hive, the tiny, slowing vessels jive,
Leaving wakes;
Seagull wheels.
The sad river chokes with leaves and Earth, ironically,
As Big Ben chimes out, through the evening, on dusk's
Ringing airwaves, at seven,
Grey night falls.

Andrew Stephenson

Surrey – Small And Special

Among most special countries in these isles,
One smaller one gets smaller from prime thought,
Now steal more land and seize it for those files,
Great Wen of swelling monster grabs for naught,
Accept more land indulging constant urge,
Expansion helps tax purpose and great vice,
Of making London wealthy with vast surge.'
Poor England suffers greatly from device,
Of over-government and constant claims,
For overriding lordship some desire,
To make their self-importance achieve aims,
While peasants, left in Surrey, tend heath fire.
One cause perhaps does save us with renown,
World's greatest race gives Epsom its own crown.

Now Shakespeare went from Stratford, as you've heard,
Aspiring 'earn a crust' in scribbled ways,
Great London would agree was not absurd,
'They might be entertained' with blank-verse plays,
Provided he removed himself each night,
To Southwark, then in Surrey, which provides.
Room for those would-be writers of delight,
Who were not college-trained or Oxford 'Brides
Of Scholarship' acclaimed compulsory
These days! How sad it was just then to fear,
All penalties promoting vanity,
Surrounding court and commoners – we hear –
While Queen of such survivors from long wars,
Desired much entertainment and applause.

Those ferments of loved words from Southwark's grime,
Do serve to warm-up Cobbett and real 'Rides',
Across most southern counties – not by rhyme –
But honesty of purpose which confides,
Intelligence fast-shrinking from these shores,
Where no one much believes in anything.

Poor Surrey does seem baffled by these chords,
We have to suffer greatly from youth's spring,
Where people seldom know and never speak,
Bemused by rich explosions everywhere,
Financially from Syria to Greece,
Like over-laden camels of despair,
Wide-world presents us daily in our lives,
Where Surrey humbly prays and just survives.

Anthony John Russell

Nature Knows Best

The utter bleakness of cold, wintry days
adds to the sheer dank heaviness,
all dead, decaying and definitely lifeless.

Then, a subtle climate change,
suddenly and miraculously
my spring semi-wild cottage garden becomes
a gentle serenade of buzzing, humming life.

Perfumes flood around in the enticing air
as winter honeysuckle and daphne bring
beautiful, breathtaking magic.
After the astonishing aconite awakening so yellow, so silent,
snowdrops shyly appear.
Stillness all forgotten now with birdsong around.

In the afternoon sunshine Nature embraces the whole scene
and many tiny brave shoots already seen.
Our hearts thrill to the sight of a sea of crocus
and primroses emerging under the hedge.
Hyacinths bring pure delight and Christmas roses coyly hold their own,
Yes, Nature knows best,
as our countryside in Kent reveals.

Margaret Ann Wheatley

ODE TO THE DOWNLANDS

Snuggled in the South Downs in the hills I know so well,
Are the glories of old England with many a tale to tell.
For long before computers, television and the like;
Before we hopped on trains and planes and even rode a bike;
We surely had a story, which was then the modern way;
And no one ever thought there'd be the things we have today.

It is with joy I visit, to see the horse and cart,
The pottery, the carpentry and countless works of art,
The views that stretch out far beyond, even to the sea,
The feelings that come flowing, of how life used to be.
The old village of Singleton . . . that is the place for me.

Jill Harding

THE GARDEN OF ENGLAND

I viewed the vista there before me
Of fields and orchards colourful and bright,
Such beauty shared with anyone who dared
To cast an eye and there peruse the sight.

Apples, pears and fruits of numerous kinds
Kissed by the sun and ripened by its rays,
Perpetuating year by year each season's yield,
To satisfy Man's needs for many days.

Beyond the orchards, fields of golden corn
A glorious spectre, upright, proud and strong,
Adjacent to broad meadows lush and green
With sheep and lambs in an abundant throng.

No wonder as one overlooked this picturesque scene
One could not but enjoy the beauty here displayed,
As all whose privilege it was to browse
Upon such loveliness the Garden of England so arrayed.

John Pert

God's Glory

Classical music and poetry can be so heavenly
When it's filled with God's glory
So inspiring, and so enchanting
It's there for all to see.
Thus filled with art, embracing one's heart
For this is truly eternal
It lives forever ours to remember
For this is so spiritual.
So filling us with love, from God above.
As this is His creation
If we speak to God, listening to His word
In prayer that he does mention.
This music written, is never forgotten
Its majesty states God's holy word in truth
Choral or symphony or piano melody
So inspiring when heard His proof,
To compose a sonnet in rhyme so perfect
A love sonnet we will always remember
About a loved one, about love you have won
In one's mind forms an enchanting picture
Or words in prose, which shows
Life's true realistic meaning
About the way we live, and what we give
To the reader what is showing.
What is known. This cannot be achieved on ones own.
For God is guiding the way
He only asks of you, that you be true
And spend time with Him to pray.
Remember what's been given, words truly spoken
From our Saviour the love of Christ
From Calvary to victory
This is what we should remember most.

Leon Gould

Thick As A Brick

Continually chattering away about TV Land
EastEnders, X Factor and Strictly Come Dancing
The Occupational Therapists with their adoring clients
Whilst the old ladies cackle loudly over their coffee in publand.

Fast cars driven by angry louts
Not bothered about the speed limit or pedestrians
Trying to cross at the zebra.

Drunken yobs in the eerie town centre
Fighting and spewing up
After watching yet another Premiership punch-up
In the bar of shouting

'You all right then?' says the cashier
At the local supermarket
To the health conscious, politically correct mother
With screaming spoilt brats.
Then the mother and the cashier
Embark on a conversation
About school places for students
Who want to study media studies
Whatever that might be.
They nag on for half an hour.

A traffic warden, officious in nature
whose job appears to be his hobby
Hands out a ticket for incorrect parking
In a parking space.

The Middle East
another revolution, more people killed.
London – more riots.
When you're a student
The police will kick your head in
But when you graduate
They will sympathise with your economic situation
And stand and do nothing.

Airport security
As paranoid as hell since 9/11
Like little Hitlers
As though they're gonna hit you.

Unscramble my brain
Make sure it's as sharp as hell,
Never lame, never as thick as a brick.

Matthew Lee

Sussex-By-The-Sea

From my open window the Downs are close
Forecasting rain is on the way.
Soon it will sweep across the towns and meadows
Quickly returning to the chalk cliffs
Hence sweeping out to sea . . .
This varied landscape which houses Man and beast
Conceals a chequered history –
Ancient incursions bequeathing a pattern
Of Iron Age tools and fossils;
The surge of Spitfires mingled with the sound of guns.
Forever returning to an even rhythm.

Encroaching dwellings spread
Where Southdown sheep once grazed
And farmland reigned supreme.
Still there are secluded corners
Where pheasants vaunt and orchids thrust defiant heads;
Meadows where lavish growth has dwarfed the deer,
Whose young are just a shudder in the grass;
Where giant oak have weathered many storms.
Shrouding, chalk-filled Downs
Breathe in refreshing breezes from the sea . . .

Veronica Charlwood Ross

A Gastronomic Tour Of Kent

A gastronomic tour of eating places found in Kent
To give you entertainment just as much as nourishment
Might begin, if you are shrewd, in your desire to sample food,
By setting on your journey from the Medway town of Strood.

And if you're really looking for some good exotic cooking
With the courses spiced with sauces, in a sumptuous, slap-up meal
Then perhaps an arty party on the ancient Isle of Harty
Will whet you growing appetite before you go to Seal.

But don't forget to hurry on to Sturry for a curry,
Or to Welling where they're Selling some tandoories that are hot,
And diners will be drooling at a restaurant in Cooling
That is serving up some gateaux richly topped with apricot.

Across the way at Yalding there's a pub where soup is scalding
And the rolls are all pre-buttered though I cannot tell you Wye;
While if you go to Chilham with your jam jars you can fill 'em
With the most delicious marmalade before you leave for Leigh.

The jellies made in Marden take a little while to harden
While in Shoreham people pour 'em into fancy plastic moulds;
These are rare but one can sight 'em if you wander on to Ightham
And can measure out the quantity that each container holds.

There's a snack bar out at Minster run by such a smashing spinster
Whose food is fresh and crisp because she keeps it in the fridge;
Taking bread in either hand which, with some ham, she makes a Sandwich
You can munch before meandering upon your way to Bridge.

If it's grouse you want then Wrotham is the place where gypsies shoot 'em
For they poach 'em there and cook 'em in a vessel with a Lydd;
But sometimes they will hawk 'em by the brace to folk in Fawkham
Or cart 'em off to Chartham, where they sell for seven quid.

And if you are a glutton for your mutton go to Sutton
To a restaurant on the corner that is on the road to Deal;
But you may prefer an evening, sampling soufflés close to Chevening
Or at Manston where there's Branston for your pickle with cold veal.

Some restaurants are pricey and, for diners, very dicey;
Owners sting 'em out at Wingham and they do the same at Oare;
In West Malling they're appalling and I've met 'em worse in Petham
And you'll fault 'em in Waltham where they charge you even moiré.

FORWARD POETRY REGIONALS 2012 - SOUTHERN ENGLAND

Before your journey's over drive your Rover down to Dover
Where there's masses of fresh fish, such as the local sole and plaice;
You can try 'em there or buy 'em and return by way of Higham;
When you're home, it's best to fry 'em, though to steam is no disgrace.

The pies they make in Gillingham have lots of fillings, filling 'em,
Folk scoff 'em down in Offham in a pub beside a field,
While gourmets out at Milton, end their meal with port and stilton
And a brandy comes in handy after dinner up at Weald.

We must finish, now, with eating as this poem needs completing
And the inspiration for it is so evidently spent,
But if anyone retraces this itinerary of places
They are sure of satisfaction at the restaurants of Kent.

T J Schaeffer

WINTER SEA

The grey winter sea and sad ochre beach,
Lone footprints trail across the virgin sand.
Cold sun bleeding weakly through hazy cloud,
Sending its torch-like beams
Down upon this vacant scene.
A vastness
Whose horizon belies the Earth's curvature.
Groynes flagged in seaweed,
Beach huts standing to attention
Empty now.
Dogs meet in their sniffing, playful way
Then run back to the sea again,
The grunting master's call disobeyed.
All is at one as it has ever been.

Jimmy Hamilton

THE GARDEN OF ENGLAND

My county is Kent
A lifetime I've spent
Within her boundaries
Forging precious memories

Kent, the garden of England
Just one corner of our island
With famous cliffs and scenic coasts
Verdant land, dotted with oasts

Battles raged overhead
In war torn Kent, we watched in dread
Our white cliffs and Vera Lynn
Were symbols that helped us win

Kentish people have known fame
Many have a famous name
Like Charles Dickens, known worldwide
And Dame Kelly, with her golden pride

The Darling Buds of May
Are remembered to this day
The garden of England, wild and free
Kentish beauty for all to see

Even now with motorway
And Channel Tunnel, here to stay
The beauty of Kent can still be seen
From white cliffs to Downs so green

Jean Everest

SUSSEX BY THE SEA

Whether it be sun-drenched beaches,
Sparkling chalk cliffs to climb,
The best of Sussex cream teas on offer –
You'll always find a welcome
Here at Sussex by the sea.

The views from Bexhill's glorious De La Warr
Both inspire and fascinate –
Miles of sand at each low tide
Beckon the tiny paddler; beachcomber and fisher-folk
Discovering what nature's perfect playground can provide.

Wendy Whitehead

Eastern Promise

East Anglia in dawn's morning heralds
A chorus of birdsong low and high
Open Broads reflecting bright sunlight
Echoes of trilling skylarks fill your sky
A panorama of dormant beauty add
Scenes of pristine wonder on virgin ground
While creatures of the wildwoods
Bathe in sunlight in mystical peace now found.

East Anglia in evening's sunset
Skies painted red and pink aglow
Silhouetting rooks and circling wildfowl
Soaring in thermals they climb and go
A windswept orchestra of reed beds
Whispering sweet music to our ears
Gentle breezes kiss still waters
While expanding ripples catch our tears.

East Anglia in early springtime
Creates new landscapes of red and blue
Wooded glades carpeted by bluebells
Adding majestic splendour to our view
Dog rose and violet fritillary butterfly silently glides by
A spotted woodpecker's resonant drumming
Echoes from silver birch and fills the sky.

East Anglia in late Autumn
Where golden leaves fall thick and still
Many Kaleidoscopes of changing colours
Give a new identity of nature's will
Fresh hues and shades in vast wildwoods
Heralds in a distinctive day
Like the autumn of our own lives
Holding a different meaning along the way.

Jim Wilson

Minster (Mynstre)

I have been asked to write about the village in which I live.
To express the warm welcome our villagers give.
To all and sundry from far and wide.
Also to say we are surrounded by beautiful countryside.
Minster-in-Thanet is steeped in history from centuries gone by.
We have a delightful church and steeple which from all points meets the eye.
We also are proud to tell all that in our village and ancient abbey stands.
Not far from the actual place where St Augustine did land.
It is said the saint baptized his first two converts in the dyke that flows in the Durlock area,
This I have read.
Also the name of our village was once spelt Mynstre,
Derived from the first monastery built in 670, gosh,
I have so much in my head.
From the top of our hill can be seen so much,
Things so close one could feel they could touch.
King William III it is said, resorted to Prospect Hill, for the magnificent view.
Five churches, the tower of Canterbury Cathedral and other sights too.
Reculver Towers, the coast of France, and much pretty land
I can tell you this is true, seen by myself at first hand.
We have roman villa foundations hidden beneath our Earth,
We have Saxon burials, and for what it is worth,
I once held an oyster shell in my hand,
As I stood in the enclose of the Roman villa foundation,
And for this I did not need to search.
Hengist, who founded the Kingdom of Kent, and Horsa, landed a few miles away.
At a place named Ebbsfleet, and more I must say.
Roman Galleys used to sail the Wantsum River, that made us an isle,
I could go on and on and on, perhaps I should pause for a while.
Oh no! We have a road named Watchester, which was once called The Drove.
Where Roman soldiers used to march from the fort seen on our horizon at Rutupia, to Canterbury City,
This city once named Duravernum, and now wouldn't it be a pity.
If I did not add here I visit Canterbury Cathedral every week;
To visit St Thomas Beckett's murder site
Thinking whilst there of Henry II's plight.
After he had uttered the famous words, 'Will no one rid me of this turbulent priest,'
I stand there thinking words in my head, 'Are you friends in Heaven now, perhaps pals at least.
I must begin to complete these lines, by adding we have much wildlife about us too.
Swans, ducks, moorhens, squirrels, birds of many varieties, and in spring they visit of the bird who calls *Cuckoo*.
So take note, friendly folk, lovely restaurants, cafes and pubs.
Shops and a helpful doctor's surgery, and as I say many places for good grub.

Buses and trains to get us around.
We have everything anyone could desire on need, on Minster's ground.
Just finish by saying two more things,
Our children have great schools here for the time when their education begins.
Our village sign shows the hind – which in itself tells of much history.
I cannot write more, now so I shall leave this as a mystery.
I feel I should change my mind, and tell you about the famous white hind.
It is widely believed, around 670 AD, whether in truth or legend
May or may not be, that the hind emblem owes its origin to Egbert, King of Kent
And Princess Domneva, married to this gent.
The king asked Domneva which piece of land she wished to take,
In compensation for the murder of her two brothers, what of this do you make?
Her answer was that she would take no more than her hind would run around
This the king granted her with pleasure, and the land became Minster ground.

Yvonne Chapman

The Installation Of The New Vice-Chancellor

Today the dons who teach at Cambridge
installed their new VC
like I install some newish software
into my old PC

Sir Les marched down the Senate House
just like my CD drive;
the only real difference is
the VC's (just) alive!

His beadle in 'attract-mode' led
Sir Les, in case you missed him,
who was followed by his 'marshal' whose
a sort of back-up system . . .

. . . and all the congregation wore
their mortar board square hats
which are the patterns stenciled on
my software's free mouse mat.

His installation then involved
the laying on of hands
with babbled incantations like
my PC's blurred commands!

William Greig

Kent In Springtime

The river, grey, fast-flowing and quite choppy,
The blue horizon, giving us signs,
Of good weather ahead.
Fields, surrounding both sides of the river,
Presenting a picture of a chequered
Carpet of different colours.

Trees, growing side by side,
And yet totally different
Both in shape, colour and height.
These majestic trees, some so high
That it is difficult, to even see their tops.
Other trees, growing opposite each other
Meet in the middle
To form an archway.

Scenes, like these are familiar
Throughout the Kent countryside
To me, these are the scenes
That fill me, with a sense of calmness,
Peace and tranquility.
In fact, I often think
It's impossible, for even a painter
To capture, a whole scene in one picture.

Maude Kiddie

Looking Into The North Sea, Kent

Where the thistle showed its purple head –
A long stem out of the turf,
And the gorse shook on the windy hill
With the surge of the distant surf,

The hills looked to the far north
And northward flowed the sea
And with the south wind on my hands
Came wonderment for me.

And there were flowers I could see
On the grass and on the spray
But the sweetest flower that caught my eye
Was the daisy flower in May.

Nola Small

Kent Coast

There is a white horse on a hill,
Above the rolling fields,
The shuttle that passes is never still,
As the speed begins to build.
A hop and a skip and you've left the coast,
Going through a tunnel, not on a ferry boat,
Off to France to see the sights,
Ooh la la – bon voyage.
Leaving behind the cliffs of white,
For a baguette filled with soft fromage,
Catch a ferry back to shore,
Why not go up on deck.
Sailing into the home I adore,
Carrying my bottle of demi-sec.

Nikki Robinson

Essex

Essex, my Essex, who dares to malign
This seat of power through all the ages past,
A bastion of freedom for all men
Who hold their heritage to England fast.

Fields and meadows lush with verdant hue
Spread all around whilst in the village there
Ship-lap cottages with willful thatch
And roses in abundance scent the air.

With forests deep and wide for all to share
Or marshlands where the curlew shrills
Nature's riches bountifully bestowed
Silver rivers and the friendly hills.

From bustling city and the market town
To havens where the weary heart might rest,
These gentle people but the first to rise
When England needs her bravest and her best.

All from this great county truly born
And Essex squires, I bid you stand and then
Raise your glass to toast this Essex fair,
And shame the comments of less noble men.

P Pidgeon

A Changed Community

As I pass the Catholic church
Upon this splendid morn
Encouraged by the sunshine
I glimpse a daisy lawn

There are lovely trees and flowers
A silver birch I see
And the blossoms are quite perfect
On the ornamental tree

Across the road the chestnut trees
All tall and stately grow
Beneath them in the border
Shrubs make quite a pleasant row

We once had HMV in Hayes
Well know, it's factories
It sold TVs, and radios
Great were its companies

We had a Regent Theatre
An Odeon we had too
Nice restaurants and better shops
It's not the Hayes we knew

We lost our lovely library
And more I have to tell!
A pool replaced our Botwell Green
Hayes Post Office as well

There's a change in our community
Seen in town these days
We've become quite multi-racial
It's a very different Hayes

When passing by the Catholic Church
Nice weddings there have been
And trees and flowers and daisy lawns
Can compensate 'twould seem

An Annigoni painting
Hangs in church for all to see
They know it has been painted
With great skill – professionally!

Life-sized – it is a painting
Of Christ upon the Cross
If ever it were stolen
'twould constitute a loss!

'Twas donated by the artist
to the church some years ago
for a religious painting
then! – what better place to go?

The painting has great value
And most Catholics they would say
They're fortunate to have it
When they kneel in church to pay

I reside here at the crossroads
Most toxic is the air
The traffic builds up constantly
For health there's little care!

Hayes has a botanical garden
And a wildlife park to view
A bowling green quite close to town
And a leisure centre too.

Nice cafes – or a restaurant
Seem popular these days
And those that have been opened
Get well patronised in Hayes

There's trees and shrubs in borders
Flower beds to see
Which give the town some character
And improve it visibly.

I've lived here now for many years
This corner well suits me
I garden – and when I'm inspired
I still write poetry!

Sylvia Russell

THAT SURREY TREE

(This is written about a tree opposite my bedroom window in a field opposite our family house in Slipsnatch Road, Woodhatch, Reigate, Surrey. It is the last road before countryside and I see our street as the last piece of urban development before rural Surrey and her villages take over.)

That Surrey tree,
stark and bare now
before March winds,
has stood there
watching through
all my seventy years.

In rain and snow and sun
its angular limbs
and green-leafed shade
have been a haven
for the ordinary birds
who have withstood
their hedgerow's brutal culling
though surely soon Surrey's
green parakeets will discover
its magnificence.

Today, as yesterday,
it sees in the distance
the blue Surrey hills
which lift our hearts
as season follows season
highlighted by that tree.

That Surrey tree,
centuries ago part of the Weald,
no longer now views
the Italian POWs
tilling the fields below,
nor cows grazing,
for grass lies fallow
as tonight – both to
irritate and invite –
Benson's travelling fairground
roots itself in an enclave
on the field's further edge.

That Surrey tree
has seen it all – the ebb and flow
of sedate suburban lives,
towering above nature
and above time as tomorrow
Sunday church bells ring,
the priest offers
the bread and wine for all
and residents of the street
continue, as they have
these past affluent, challenging years,
to live in virtual solitary splendour
like that tree.

Brian Frost

Over Beachy Head

The sun was warm
As we left our bed
And packed a flask
With some buttered bread
The view was fine
We were newly wed
What a wonderful dawn
Over Beachy Head

    When I reflect
    On the things we said
    When our past
    Was still ahead
    The life we planned
    On those chalky beds
    Covered with corn
    Over Beachy Head

        Now Autumn's come
        As green, brown and red
        Meet the blue sea
        White gulls overhead
        Our plans came to little
        Despite all that we said
        But I love you still
        Over Beachy Head.

Stuart Delvin

ONE HOT AFTERNOON IN JUNE

(A walk on the Hurtwood)

The wood is vibrant with voices,
Stems stir, insects hum in the air,
Rabbits rustle in the undergrowth.
There is a battering in the trees, of bees,
As they seek the succulent pollen of tall oaks,
On this one, hot afternoon in June.

A wood pigeon, startled by footsteps,
From its feed on the seed of sycamore and lime,
Bludgeons its way, awkwardly, to the branch of the pine.

The sunlight drops, pendulously, through the lattice-leaf roof,
Spilling golden sovereigns
On the damp, peaty soil of the forest floor,
Indiscriminately
On this one, hot afternoon in June.

A jay jabs the silence, cracking the air, jarringly,
Over the bracken frond-fringed pool in the forest
A breeze murmur whispers over the surface of the water,
Ruffling it.
Beneath, in the wet world of water weed and snails
A fish fin flickers almost imperceptibly.

I walk on with soft footsteps,
Intensely aware of the burr and the stir of living things
On this one, hot afternoon in June.

Jane Finlayson

WHAT HAS EASTBOURNE TO OFFER?

An Edwardian town, offering theatres,
The Towner Art Gallery and Princess Park.
The sun, the sea and all the societies
To which you could belong.
The pier, promenade and bandstand
Are second to none.
Have I mentioned the flowers?
No? The Carpet Gardens are a delight.

Elizabeth Jenks

Dawn, September, Southwold

The eastern skies smear pale blue to yellow.
The waves gently rumble the stones about.
The houses on the cliff are dark, fighting the clock.
A stray seagull scratches its wing feathers,
while balancing on a breakwater.

The blue-black night retreats westwards,
as the sun forces her way out through the sea.
Yellow turns to pink and reds.
A homecoming fishing boat flashes in the light.
The silence stretches itself and, yawning, leaves.

The first commuter's car departs for the early train.
The dustmen clatter their way along the front.
Bacon sizzles in guesthouse kitchens,
and my second cup of tea grows cold in the sunlight,
as I watch the tiny rollers surfing in.

At this time of day the eternal questions drift by,
more smoothly than the ice cream papers of later hours.
The meaning of life; the challenge of the times;
how much I love them; how can I stay
and whether or not I shall swim today?

David W Lankshear

Horizon Line (East Coast)

Sun never set in more changeable seas
Or distance and light set the landscape free
Where sunsets seem to encompass the world
As expansive skies and distance unfurl . . .
Where wild winds batter coastal piers
And surging waves reach new frontiers . . .
Nowhere on Earth does life give birth
With greater sadness or joyful worth,
Where intimate corners shield the seed
To shingled coasts that challenge the deed . . .
Where sea and sky are the ultimate cry
On the wings of gull as it flashes by
And the songs and sins of our forefathers spin,
On the fishermen's nets at sunset's rim . . .

Colleen Biggins

The Fields Of Sussex

The fields of Sussex are very strange,
The chief ones number four,
There are green fields and brown fields,
Yellow fields, and plastic fields what's more.

The green fields are grass, and when ready
The mowers are brought in to cut it.
This then turns to hay for feed and bedding
For animals and birds who love it.

The cattle and sheep are then put
Into these green fields to graze,
To enjoy the new grass that has grown,
And will do so for a great many days.

The brown fields have been ploughed
Ready for sowing wheat or maize,
These crops will then be harvested
For animal feed during the winter days.

The yellow fields only appear in the spring
When the oil-seed rape is widespread.
When the golden petals drop, the seeds are gathered
To help make your 'low fat' spread.

The 'plastic' fields are very modern and prominent,
I wonder if they yield cling film or freezer bags?
Or shopping bags, yoghurt pots, or beakers?
Or maybe rain hats, milk containers or food bags.

I've not yet witnessed the harvesting
Of products these 'plastic' fields grow
No doubt it is something useful, but
I don't expect we will ever know!

Judith Herrington

CHURCH OF HAVEN

(St Margaret's Lower Halstow – An 1806 visit by S T Coleridge)

This church of haven
small and curious
snug by the quayside
at Lower Halstow;
empty and open
safe from tidal flow.

The church of haven
silently invites
the returned poet
silent and alone;
familiar wind
the shelter of home.

The church of haven
silently becomes
a muse for retreat
in which Man can hide;
salvation reborn
life identified.

Lone church of haven
reuniting time
the silent poet
his travels unknown;
a mountainside col
for us now – is home.

Alan Dickson

City Of My Dreams

Through the mists of time her beauty shines,
My city of dreaming spires sublime.
She is the fairest of all the shires,
The one of which I'll never tire.

Steeped in history, it's Oxford for which my mind is ever yearning,
This ancient seat of eternal learning.
The 21st century is making its mark,
Although there is an easy escape to one of her beautiful parks.
And maybe watch a game of cricket,
This, my friend, is just the ticket.

The botanical gardens are such a joy,
Punts on the river gently gliding by.
With sunlight glinting on ripples in their wake,
In a dream of 'Alice in Wonderland' it's so easy to partake.

The tradition of May Morning is a wonder to behold,
At a very early hour, choirboys with sweet voices sing on Magdalen Tower.
Then Morris dancers entertain us with jingling bells and the cracking o their sticks,
Usually accompanied by a jolly accordionist.
I was born and bred in Oxford and here I'll always stay,
I will never leave her and travel far away.

Val Bermingham

My Neighbourhood

We meet up in the library or at the U3A
Or sometimes at the TG upon another day
On Sundays at the church we meet, or sometimes in the week
When we are doing shopping and there are friends to greet.
Taking grandkids to the school door there's a friendly group like us
Or the pleasant folk who'll give their seat when getting on the bus
Those folk whose volunteering runs all the charity shops
Have a pleasant smile just like the one of the uniformed police cops
The place may not be so beautiful or have the finest scene
But it's generally well cared for and the place is always clean.
So it's not down to the geography when put up to the test
It's the people in our borough that simply make it best.

Ron Morris

THE SUSSEX DOWNS

Over the rolling Sussex Downs
There can be seen for miles around
Cornfields waving in the breeze
The magic that the eye perceives,
And the wildlife in abundance there
Just walk the Downs and take the air.

Look yonder as you travel onward.
In the distance lies the sea.
Enjoy all this, taste every moment –
The windswept beauty wild and free
Scattered hamlets of brick and flint,
Nestling low twixt dip and brow –

The charm and the beauty of the Southern Downs,
The neat little villages and country towns.
The winding Cuckmere, the humpty bridge,
The Smuggler's Rest, grand views from the ridge
As you stand to survey, in the fresh sweet air, –
England's glory is everywhere.

Pamela Dean

A BLUEBELL WOOD

The wood was a place enchanting
Seen through the tree trunks nigh –
Lit by the sunbeams slanting,
Earth seemed paved with the sky.

Bluebells massed by the million –
A carpet of marvellous hue
Under the green pavillion
Spread in a glory of blue.

Sapphire, and sax, and royal,
From azure to indigo deep,
But always to blueness loyal,
Like Fairyland seen in sleep.

Pure beauty is joy without leaven –
Dimly I understood,
I had opened a path to Heaven
By a glance in a bluebell wood.

Henry Harding Rogers

PUREST LOVE

Arriving, white ribboned, chauffeured car
At Park Plaza, River Bank Hotel, London Embankment
Reception, adorned Union Jack giant cups, saucers, red, white blue flowers
Lady registrar, backing Parliament, Westminster
Reads, the couple's format

Room scented, with balled white roses, thistles, lavender flowers
Vows, seriously exchanged
Applauded, champagne uncorked
Photographer capturing, scenic venue
Special guests, presentation, silver case

Garden restaurant, canapés, champagne
Silver service dinner, under candlelight
Starched tablecloths, napkins, white roses, thistles, lavender, flowers adorning
Profiteroles and chocolate cake cut
Chauffeured driven home

Memories of a golden day
Happy couple, watching diamond jubilee
Later, travelling to Italy
Enjoying, beauties of Florence
May, peace, perfecting love, be with you both.

Patricia Turpin

SUMMER IN KENT

It's good to be home in Kent again
After months in sunnier climes
Where the raucous, rasping, screech of birds
Rends the breathless, listless, air;
Where the sun bores down with relentless force
And night's release is balm

Yes it's good to walk in the woods again
To the blackbird's melodious song;
With the fragrant scent of new-mown grass
On the gentle summer breeze;
And a robin hops along the path
With cheeky, fearless glance
And a squirrel scampers for cover, yet curious
Peeps round the bole of a tree.

Alan Compton

A Pigeon's Eye View

As I fly the streets of Sutton
I can see them down in the street
Loads of people shopping
Plenty of places to eat.

Markets in the High Street
Bargains you cannot believe
'Scuse me while I'm landing
I can see a cake to retrieve.

Buses and trains to serve you
To the coast, the country, the Queen,
I've seen it all believe me
'Scuse me, I've just seen an ice cream.

It's time for me to stop talking
And get back home for my tea
Did you say that your cake is stale?
Could it possibly be for me?

Brenda Bartlett

Edinburgh Tour

The time will pass then very soon
We'll a' gang up tae Auld Reekie toon
A city tour or shopping marts
Or a fitba' match between Hibs and Hearts

The castle atop and the palace below
The Royal Mile puts on quite a show
There's Princes Street and its lovely garden
A perfect place to read the Bard in (Robbie Burns of course)

And with our wives a little banter
About should we wear a Tam o' Shanter
And at our age 'twould be a feat
To climb the towering Arthur's Seat

Into the air we'll jump as one
When they fire the One O'Clock Gun
In sunshine or in silver moon
I know you'll love Auld Reekie toon.

David Macaulay

Furrows

Everywhere you look
in the nature of time,
are patterns and forms
and rows of lines:

Long narrow trenches
in the ground from plough;
arable farms walked once
by muddy sows.

The long deep grooves
we call wrinkles,
on permanently worried
or ageing brows.

Prospective fruits
of laboured hours,
in seed-drilled furrows
with veggie towers.

We look around
and see beside,
our eyes cast down
and nature hides –
the beauty performed
in tests of time;
nature's everywhere –
in spills of lines.

Phoebe Carter

This Ragged Glen

And so I came in awe to gaze upon
This proud and mighty crag
Took a ragged ride to Heaven's door
Through the glen of a cruel hag . . .
Saw the mighty Carrauntoohil
Unrivalled King of Kerry's reeks
A humbling devil of a mountain
Tumbled raw from fearful steeps . . .

Stood at the edge of a shallow world
I took a step into a primitive age
Took my place in a valley where Man
Is at the mercy of nature's rage . . .
Of a fearsome rage in Heaven
A cruel war between rock and sky
I held my breath and stole a glance
Crossed my heart and cared not if I died!

And so I came in dread to understand
This dour and dreadful rock
To scale the devil's ladder to Hell itself
And whatever door I chose to unlock
Spied the mighty Carrauntoohil
Tallest stone in this storied glen
A gateway at the end of he world
Ripped ragged from the hearts of men!

Stood at the end of this famine road
I left my footprint in the hungry grass
Stole a stone and one last fearful look
From this barren – broken past
A past steeped in greater glories
The relentless turmoil between rain and fire and stone
I held my breath and said one last prayer
Then called this ragged glen my home . . .

Mike Goddard

Take Me Back

There's a ripple on the water
and sunshine on the waves,
The White Cliffs of Dover
just turn us into slaves.
I need that ball and chain again
to relax a bit and think,
Build castles in the air
where nothing's ever new;
just water, water, everywhere
with not a drop to drink.
The magic of the ferries
you can see, but never hear,
a silent movie, simple life,
with sea and sky so near,
Far-flung beaches, gull and cliff,
No limits to my thoughts,
Perfect reflections raise a tear
as many times before,
So wing me back where bluebirds fly
and let me smell the sea once more!

Alan Smith

Birhington Cliff Top Walks

Early morning walk,
Where the dew is in the air
Seagulls' cries high,
Above the cliff tops.
Where the seagulls hide.
Silent as the grave.
All is at peace, As the world sleeps.
The wild flowers peeping out over the cliff tops.
Sea waves silent,
Coming into the shore.
Sun lights up the sky,
Aglow is everywhere.
No other peace to be found,
But to walk the cliff tops on high.
No other place,
Where the seagulls cry.

Iris Davey

My Utopia (Wonderful Thing)

Hearts beating, heavy breathing,
Feet shuffling, muffled speaking,
None of us truly know how we feel
Caffeine fuelled and aggravated
The faceless street walkers' stance never changes
The pristine sidewalk has been burdened
By shuffling shoes and cigarette butts
And old pieces of bubblegum
To clear the streets of London
Would be an infinite career
Words I'd never utter in fear
Of the city hearing me
What of the slurred speech?
(My bid to change the course of this talk)
I ask the pavement such silly queries
What of the acquaintance we've lost
'Keep in touch' being the last thing the forgotten person asked of you
Yes, keep in touch, we must
For a week – and then you'll turn into a fading memory
What of the faintest whisper in the wind
The breeze caressing your cheeks
As you lay in the grass
Surrounded by Earth and forestry
I ask and ask and wonder why
The pavement never once did reply
What of the boats – all shapes and sizes – parked,
On the edges of the River Thames
Not once did I see them do what they were built for
Set sail and take people to their destinations.
What of the parts of this great city
That I truly have come to appreciate
Doused in history – the likes of . . .
Charles Dickens and Vincent Van Gogh
Living in the areas I grew up in
What a wonderful thing to know.

Naima Artan

From An Open Window In Sussex

I look out of the window,
and what do I see?
Birds landing on branches
up in the tree.

There are blackbirds, starlings,
great tits and blue,
sparrows, collared doves,
green and gold finches too.

Some feeding their young
with beaks full of food.
Working so hard
for their hungry brood.

Gathering from seeders
and down on the ground,
their wings gently flapping
making a wonderful sound.

Onto the bird table
for a different treat,
then spying a cat
and making a hasty retreat.

Soon they are back
only minutes have passed
most probably knowing
their peace won't last.

Then feasting on fat balls
I can't believe me eyes
a great spotted woodpecker,
what a surprise.

His colours so vivid
black, white and red,
then he flies off
high over the shed.

Next a red admiral
comes fluttering by,
rests on the honeysuckle
and then back up in the sky.

For a moment it's quiet,
there's no noise around
then suddenly I hear
a loud buzzing sound.

Is it a fly
or a wasp maybe?
No, it's a beautiful
bumblebee.

Its colours so striking,
black and bright gold,
this really is
a sight to behold.

It comes and lands
on a lovely pink rose
off onto a white lily
then away it goes.

In the pergola corner
a spider spinning away
making its web
to trap all its prey.

At the garden's end
the fields are so green,
and the sheep and cows
can clearly be seen.

The hedges are growing
row upon row,
and horses are galloping
you should see them go.

The farmers in tractors
never seem to stop,
a couple more months
and they'll be cutting the crop.

The west Sussex hills
are touching the sky
and white fluffy clouds
go floating by.

The afternoon sun
is shining so bright,
flooding the land
with its warmth and light.

I can see God's love
in all of this
because without Him
nothing exists.

Teresa Mary Street

THANET

Acres, no, miles of growing things,
Propagating under cover,
Stretches of green,
Country lanes and endless rings
Of houses almost to the sea,
And over all a big blue sky seen,
With glorious multicoloured suns
Rising and setting on the so flat fields.
Now gone, the cooling towers,
Those great and gently sloping things,
A coastline, rugged cliffs and countless birds free-wheeling in the shelter of the rocks in eddies of the
Land and sea.
And in the castle, are there guns?
And then the highway loud,
Proclaiming that this erstwhile island is not left
Behind.
And there's a gallery of art so proud,
And in the out of season bays, there is a crowd.
May Thanet grow with knowing, yet,
With green spaces, may it still be kind.

Philip Clements

Newtimber Hill

The Weald was choked in clinging murk,
The Downs stretched up, the chalky steep
Submerged in swathes of miry clay;
The trees like ghosts about my path
Let fall their droplets in my hair.
The muggy air was breathless, still,
As I climbed upward swathed in gloom;
The deadened silence wrapped me round,
No sound from birds too glum to sing.

I slithered on the slippery slope,
Then climbed the stile and left the wood
To feel my mood to lighten some.
The mist still clung to sodden grass
As I resumed my weary climb.
But suddenly the gloom was gone
And sunshine bathed the landscape, while
The golden gorse was scattered wide
And spiders strung their diamonds there.

The sky stretched round in deepest blue
With larks ecstatic, hovering there –
I revelled in this fairyland.
Below, the tower of Poynings church
Just pierced the clouds that hid the nave,
Reminder of the certain hope
That lifts the soul beyond the tomb
And out into the sunlight, where
The fresher air excites the breath.

Winter and Spring have hastened by
And Summer still extends its reign
As I climb nimbly through the shade.
The Weald below is bright and clear
And Wolstanbury bathes in light
As does the hill to westward, which
Is cleft in two by Devil's Dyke.
Silence, peace, relaxing space –
My favourite place, Newtimber Hill.

Vaughan Stone

CHELMSFORD CITY

Chelmsford, at last, is a city
though it's had a cathedral for years.
An ancient site, on a river,
that has seen many heartaches and tears.

Renowned for its inventor, Marconi –
who gave us the first taste of sound
transmitted to alter our leisure –
revolutionise all life around.

Chelmsford now sits in a patchwork
of fields, woods and quiet countryside,
licking its wounds now as factories
have slowly shut down and died.

There are still the blocks of offices
and sprawling estates just lurk
while all their hardy commuters
go up to London for work.

Like everywhere, there's a dearth there
of shops selling their unique wares.
The big-boys have most of the trade now
and stock 'the same stuff' without care.

But the bars and the pubs and theatres
give joy and entertainment alike
and there's plenty to do, for the youngsters,
who let off steam through the night.

Chelmsford's ideal for a city
and worthy of the name
for it still offers lots of variety
and deserves its new-found fame.

Fredrick West

End Of Day On The Sussex Downs

Distant glimmers of a fading sun
Reflect on solitary buildings
Smoke-tinted hills entwine
A dusky sky
Trees stand starkly
Against a fading light

No utter of breeze
Silently waiting snow clouds
Slowly approaching
To burst, engulf
With an icy white veil

No other end of day
Will be the same
As this day
Sinking gracefully
In a silent mist of snow

Pauline Ann Smith

Brentford

Cut by the Great West Road,
And Motorway Four on stilts.
And railway and canal cut.
Walking. Not driving through on the way to somewhere else.
West or east I sense your private peace.
The coming home of your railway line
The end of your England long canal opening to River.
Here the Romans crossed
And the royal coach sped through
To the soldiers on the Heath and Windsor.

The spire, reaching Heaven once,
Now is level with the road on stilts.
I know your people, or some,
The mums, the foster mother, the friend who died.
And your evening, very full, very red cars cradled
Among the speeding roads
To other homes.

James O'Grady

My Mobile Home In Winkfield

I look out of my door so bright and clean
Bright red and yellow roses climbing so tall
With lots of homes positioned around
They are all mobile homes so neat within
But they cannot move around at all
So their wheels are still and sad
With the trees so tall and grand
They seem to look down and stare
The birds singing songs to please all
Then the sound of engines starting up very near
The buses get ready for the school trip and noise
As they go into a larger town to learn
Some get on the bus so near indeed
The entrance of the local pub so large
Which is the heart of the small town today
With lots of fun and talk within
As we are so close to London right now
The talk is often varied and loud
Some prefer the town and the bustle
Others prefer the country and the quiet
While those from the polo club so near
They like the country and the noise
While I like both so I will say cheers

Brian D Ball

Village Pub

I sit alone and Stare.
Where.
Here and there
not sure I know
deep in thought
emotions flow.
Sad, happy
jolly, low.
Bottomed out now
not sure where to go.
S'pose local watering hole
is the place to go.

Thomas Baker

The Downs Of Sussex

Gazing in the distance my eyes beheld a scene,
One of sheer captivating wonders, displaying a mystical sheen,
As if Mother Nature had paused, to capture a moment
To relish and savour, as if time required appreciated atonement,

Displaying undulating impression reaching high for the sky,
Coat of green grass, groups of fine trees gently whisper a soothing sigh,
Grazing cattle one can see in the distance quietly at peace,
Solitude seems to engulf their stance, with a swishing tailpiece.

Serenity captures this awesome gift of nature's charm,
As pathways invite a quiet meander, to enjoy this element of calm,
A natural landscape to relish with pride, this glorious privilege,
Enhancing every aspect surrounding this legendary heritage.

The Downs are a spectacle with contended charisma,
A charmed vision of reality which radiates a glimmer,
Establishing a sense of peace, through the space of time,
Protecting force of nature, a gift of Neptune, through the age of time.

As each season descends upon our treasured Downs,
Each conveys a beauty, to adhere with its seasonal crowns,
Spring, summer, autumn, winter each holds a colourful gift to wear,
A treasured prize we eagerly await, and observe the adornment created to share.

Lorna Tippett

Quiet Corner

As I enter the stillness
In the slowing of pace
To be happy for freedom
For the longing of space
Of time in suspension
Is making aware
For a much simpler living
Which is calling me there
There in my moment
In the peace I receive
Is all I can wish for
In my silent reprieve.

Richard Leduchowicz

Look For Poetry

Look for poetry in Surrey,
Look, you'll find it's everywhere,
Shining on a winding river,
Rising bird-like on the air.

Autumn trees, ablaze with colour,
Like mountain flames climb up Box Hill,
Will that monstrous five-toed cockerel
Wake Pippbrook with crowing shrill?

Come with me down Dorking High Street,
Men and women, girls and boys,
Drive and cycle, walk and jostle,
Fill the street with cheerful noise.

Noise that turns to music's cadence
As you wander through the town,
Fading into gentle murmur
Where roads give way to quiet down.

Poems spring in country lanes,
Where hedgerow flowers crowd the grass,
A slender deer leaps through the bracken,
A gracious spirit, quick to pass.

There's poetry in buildings, too,
Ancient churches, stately homes,
Cottages, all black and white,
Across the fields where cattle roam.

So take your pencil and your notebook,
Look about, write what you see,
There's beauty in the Surrey landscape,
A poem in each field and tree.

Sylvia Herbert

SURBITON

'Queen of the suburbs' it used to be called,
its roads both broad and shady,
'Carriage-width' to suit the wealthy
gentleman and his lady.

No streets are here, but tree-lined closes,
avenues, drives and crescents,
With many buildings in varying styles
from Victoria's reign to the present.

Happily placed by the grand old Thames,
there are pleasant views all around,
And the railway offers convenient travel
for commuters city-bound.

It's not too far to the countryside
or a nice day out by the sea,
Theatres and shops are close to hand.
It's a popular place to be.

From the hamlet it was in days gone by
it's come such a very long way,
and developing still, new ideas, moving on,
what more is there to say?

Patricia Fallace

OUR LOVELY NEIGHBOURHOOD

Where I live, the folk are so nice
We have street parties where we dance
Our children play and cycle fast
We share jokes and have plates of grub
We borrow cups of sugar, milk
We water flowers smooth as silk
We barbecue and smell the meat
And children rejoice in their sweets
This is Crofton Park with vigour
Where rules are observed with rigour.

Muhammad Khurram Salim

Travel Through Life In Beeston

Beeston fields lie wide and open to the sky,
Home to melodious skylarks singing as they fly,
Trimmed with nodding cowslips and ladies' smock's pale hue.
Walk with me in the sunset and in the morning dew.

Kingfisher's turquoise streaking along the waterway,
Barn owl's ghostly hunting at the close of day,
Lapwing and golden plover call in at autumn's fall,
Cuckoo recites each springtime with his welcome call.

Walk along the Greensand Ridge where the bent grass sways,
On to neighbouring Northill along the Funeral Way,
Return past fields of onions and salad crops so green
To the stream and ponds and stately trees on Beeston's village green.

Sprint with me in the springtime, stroll in summer's heat,
Saunter in golden autumn, trudge in winter's sleet.
Come with me on my journey among the fields so fair,
Knowing that nature's precious gifts may always be found there.

Doreen Lawrence

Garden Time In Chiddingfold

Butterfly on buddleia, tomato on the vine,
honeysuckle, roses and lavender entwine.

Squirrel in the plum tree eating all the fruit,
blue tit on bird feeder, nuthatch follows suit.

Robin gives his perky nod as usual to me,
blackbird, thrush and sparrow – such a joy to see.

Crocosmia and sedum, cranesbill and the weeds
all live in my garden in perfect harmony.

Bumblebees are busy hanging in the air:
I am busy watching – I have time to spare!

Time to ponder world events
marvel at birdsong
everlasting pink sweet peas
hope I last as long!

Margaret E McComish

The Aylesbury Duck

If you were asked where Aylesbury got its fame,
You may not have said: 'Bucks Fizz',
Aylesbury is in Bucks, of course,
But the duck is where it is!

Of course, 'Bucks Fizz' are a marvellous group,
And we were delighted when they won
The Eurovision Song Contest – but from Bucks?
I've not idea, but they were fun.

When there happens to be duck on a menu,
Aylesbury always springs to mind,
This noble creature is the king of ducks,
To us, there is no other kind.

I've seen a menu for eastern royals
And Aylesbury Duck was there,
I've no doubt, our own royal family,
Has, at some time, sampled this fare.

Well I was born near the Aylesbury Duck Farm,
And my family knew the breeders as well,
I have a couple of toes that are webbed,
So I feel I'm an Aylesbury Duck, truth to tell!

In Aylesbury, we've no doubt many claims to fame,
But this is paramount, to me,
I was born in Mount Street, near the farm,
So an Aylesbury Duck I'll always be.

June Benton-Wright

The Greatest Of Races

On the first Saturday in June
On the undulating course of green
The most beautiful of equine beauty
Is a spectacle to be seen

With their speed and equine grace
Their thundering hooves racing
Nostrils flaring
And the determination on their sculptured faces
They compete for the most famous of races
The Epsom Derby has come to town.

The county of Surrey is green and fertile
It is a special county to work and live
And has so much life and vibrancy to give

And each year it holds the greatest of races
One that brings joy to so many faces
The Epsom Derby for all to see
This is what my county has given to me

Susan Stuart

My Village Park

We have a pretty park with flowers in bloom,
It's a riot of colour, this park is never in gloom.
There are roses, daisies, buttercups and many more,
To spend happy hours, to my park I would go,
I see the sunflowers turning, they follow the sun,
Butterflies sit on the flowers, they all have such fun,
Birds have made nests on the apple tree,
They fly where they wish, they are ever so free,
The rivulet with its gleaming waters doth glitter,
Above on the trees, the little birds twitter,
Dancing waters of the fountain in the park so green
Bring smiles to many people so often I have seen,
We see the blue sky where small clouds are sailing,
I sit in my park where peace and joy are prevailing.

Kamala Dias

Homecoming

The soft green grass is beneath my feet,
My heart it seems to miss a beat,
I'm home again, it's been so long,
The childhood memories proved too strong.

I look around and take deep breaths,
It fills my heart with happiness,
To see the old forgotten things,
Stirring my memories and my dreams.

I've roamed the world so far and wide,
Taken changes in my stride,
But nothing could stop that nagging pain,
Telling me to return again.

Months will pass, then I'll feel the urge,
To pack my bags and start to search,
For another place to settle down,
Far removed from this dear old town.

But I know that in time I'll be back again,
When my heart starts searching down memory lane,
My feet will retrace the well-worn path,
To the most wonderful place on Earth,
The land of my childhood,
The place of my birth.

Valerie Helliar

Upon East London

The East End of London is very close to the wealth of financial capital in the United Kingdom.
It is one of the poorest areas and has suffered from disadvantages and poverty.
The City of London has gained huge advantages and wealth.
The afternoon noise is barely silent.
Ships, towers, churches, domes, theatres and temples lie
Open unto the fields, and there is an aircraft in the sky.
All bright and glittering in the crisp clear air.
There is the future hope upon East London.
The area has now got the Olympic Games on their doorsteps.
It is now being awoken from its past slumbers of despair to a future legacy.

Errol Baptiste

This Scotland

This Scotland oh! the wonder of
Its form was made by God above
The beauty of the mountain heights,
With snow-cap summits – what a sight.

The crystal streams cascade and flow,
You wonder where the ripples go,
Salmon leap, fly through the air,
Young lambs dance without a care.

Lochs lie still like pools of blue
Pine trees stand so straight and true,
Sunset reddened ball of gold
Outlined hills so bleak and bold.

You can hear old history sound
Scotsmen leap over rocks and mounds,
Their flashing swords and angry yells,
How it happened – so they tell.

Tartan of all different clans,
MacKenzie, MacDonald, and MacMillan,
Reds and greens, blues and yellows,
Dirks in their belts, such fiery fellows.

This Scotland oh! the wonder of
Its form was made by God above
Made its beauty for all to see,
Every mountain, hill, valley and tree.

Margaret Davies

My Region

My region is most lovely
With woods and parks and trees
I walk along the seafront feeling each of the seasons' breezes
There's countryside and beaches
That stretch for miles so long
And of course the shopping malls that cater all day long
It's so diverse with people, a melting pot for sure
With many human beings setting off to distant shores.
Yes times have changed this lifetime
In my region and in years
But deep in heart each region is the place we all adore.

Chris Bampton

A Winter's Day At Wisley

A tapestry of colours embraces the glassy still pond,
The fiery dogwood blazes on the water's edge.
Watery rays break through the sullen clouds
And the trees stand leafless by the copper hedge.

Nodding, dancing, heads of hellebores and snowdrops
Amongst the ramrod daffodils and the curling ferns.
The musical thrush and the impatient nuthatch
Compete with all life's vibrant sounds.

The satiny dark green leaves of ivy bearing fruit
Shine as the early dew clings to the last.
The whispering sounds of dried leaves and grass
As the tiny shy mouse goes scuttling past.

The cries of soaring rooks stretching their wings
The call of comical ducks looking for their mates.
The moorhen as it plods around on spiky feet
Tells you spring will be here and it's not too late.

Margaret Lawrance

WHERE I LIVE

I live on the outskirts of a little town
Kissed on one side by a busy motorway
Where forever traffic goes up and down
The wheels of commerce turn night and day

In the town a canal with barges on
A steam train from here did ply
Now both are no more, have gone
And we ask ourselves, just why?

Under an old iron bridge, a river flows
With willow trees and duck and swan
Here two rivers merge and to the sea go on
Past towns and villages, big ships with flags upon

Cromwell's men attacked this place
The townsfolk were filled with fear
Fortifications were built apace
Cromwell's relation is buried here

Princess have been this way
Motors made for princes and kings
Samuel Pepys once here did stay
A parchment factory among other things

If you should own a cow or sheep
And a poor commoner you should be
Upon the common them you could keep
Grass aplenty for just a modest fee

Keith Coleman

MERIDIAN AT NIGHTFALL

The laser shines from Greenwich
Downhill, green and brilliant through the dusk
Due north, where does it end?
Where is the pot of gold?
And does it glow?

The beacon light speeds well from Deptford
Uphill, striving through the dust
Due east, where will it reach?
Where does the anchor hold?
How can we know?

Christopher Payne

Pride Of Place

A few miles south of Cambridge
A little north of Ware;
A dot beside a river,
That's Buntingford, look – *there!*

A pit-stop on the highway
Where travellers filled their skins
And coachmen swapped their horses
When half the shops were inns.

We haven't shrunk, like Puckeridge,
Or burgeoned, Hatfield-style.
Our shops are small and friendly.
Strangers receive a smile.

Once we were well-connected –
By road and rail, at least –
'Til Beeching axed our railway
And Green Line buses ceased;

Since when, we're part of nowhere,
And yet we're feeling great.
There's more to this old hamlet
Than maps can illustrate.

Jean Hayes

Lambeth

The beauty of London
On a summer's morn
The sound of birds
At the break of dawn

The sight of the Thames
From Lambeth Bridge
Look ye around
Splendour abounds

The beauty of London
So much to give
And so lucky am I
For in Lambeth I live

Jeanne E Quinn

Laid-Back, Easy Style

Our building, De La Warr Pavilion,
It lacks the height of many million.
Instead, it has a horizontal style,
This laid-back, easy, people's '30s pile.

Yet old and fashionably short of cash,
It needed help of late to stop a crash.
Once, often host to concerts, dances, plays,
Today, its line is modish art displays.

For these, the summer roof extends its space
Where metal figures found any airy place,
And then a beach was raised two floors,
While next a teetering coach aroused applause.

But good design prevails whatever use
Including incidental slight abuse.
A simple shape, an old familiar face,
Such things are never easy to replace.

Give thanks that Grade 2 Listing is a fact.
Let's hope it saves the De La Warr intact.
The building's kept old Bexhill well alive,
This modernist from nineteen thirty-five.

Allan Bula

My Community

My community is the place which I do love most
With one school, two shops and buses at every interval
It's vibrant, it's bold and it's colourful with beautiful houses and gardens, tall trees and hedges all around.
Our neighbourhood is always buzzing
Buzzing with kind and friendly people
People who will give a smile and a wave
With time to listen with patience and pride
A community which makes me proud.
Often from my window on a clear day
I watch the children playing games
Games of hide-and-seek, with fun and cheers
Which brings back the memories of my yesterday
For youth is the time to be jolly and brave.
My community is full of love, action, fun and laughter
Always making others welcome with a warm greeting.
Our postman never misses his delivery even on a bad weather day.
The shop assistants are always polite and friendly, with plenty of love and respect for everyone
A community which make me proud and happy.

Una Chandler

Summertime

How I wish summertime would come to stay
So I could brush the cobwebs out of the way
Flowers taking their first peek
Sunshine and petals with their warmth they seek.
Glistening with early morning dew
To awake the silent few.
Everglades so golden and green,
Such a delight to be seen
Once more the seasons come around
With all the beauty growing on the ground.

Ann Dutschak

The Charm Of Summer

The morning dew lay so soft and new
As the day dawned with a natural calm,
And the flowers glowed with nature's hue,
Enhancing all of summer's delightful charm.

And we strode out along the way
As the birds in the hedgerows burst into song,
The sun shone down and warmed the day,
Whilst love bloomed too, a feeling so strong.

Romance blossomed in the summer breeze,
Amidst sheer beauty and budding growth,
The swaying corn, the restless trees,
I reached out and embraced them both.

The radiance in my lover's smile
Caused heartbeats fast, no real sense of time,
Yet I could still tell in a little while
I would be in life's rich prime.

For she did stir within my soul
A feeling so divine and whole
That all was mine for to control,
And Heaven itself shone down upon me.

Chris Norton

BRICKS

Bedfordshire, a tiny space,
Flat, becalmed sea – still
Since ice passed this place
Lost clay has left the land no green
Robbed birds of trees, for eyes, fair seen.

Kiln cathedrals block out the sky,
Miles off, poison fumes caused trees to die.
Caverns deep, and deeper show
Earthworms venture, not to go.

The chimneys die, one by one,
Atop there is a deep dark eye,
Staring, ever upwards to the sky.
Just four are left; but not bereft.

Four proud pinnacles of LBC
From Pilgrim's house the view, I see.
I wander, as Pilgrim did
Foot-weary along the Greensand Ridge.

The Vale of Marston drifts far into mist.
The downs heave up like towering cliffs.
Bedfordshire, her heart, was taken day by day.
To build warm stalls for men to lay.

Eileen Whitmore

BEDFORD

A town of markets – the billowing canvasses
Cover a cornucopia of nature's bounteous supply.
A town of bridges – the turgid Ouse passes by
Under stone or iron or winged butterfly.
A town of flowers – hanging baskets in rainbow livery
Gardens ablaze of varied colours with tended swaths alongside.
A town of history – early settlements and power struggles
Noble men performing noble deeds with ideals of pride.
A town of learning – of schools and colleges
Climbing the demanding educational scale.
A town of languages – a veritable polyglot
An Esperanto in chrysalis form to regale.
A town of religion and reform – Bunyan and Howard
And Huddleston joining brother to brother.
A town of people – a melting pot of nations
Living together at peace with one another.
A town of hope – the future must be thought through vision
To allow its potential to gestate and expand.
A town to lead and be proud of – looking forward
Proclaiming Bedford's name throughout the land.

Robert Main

BESIDE THE SEA (BEXHILL-ON-SEA)

There is plenty to see, beside the sea
From our old Edwardian town
There's ancient and modern, side by side
And then there's the sea, with its changing tide
The countryside fields are full of golden corn
And the skies are bright in the early dawn
Old towns and villages, spread far and wide
Amid medieval castles, our history's pride
Where battles were once fought, to gain a crown
And old Tudor houses can still be found
We've a grand Pavilion built in the 1930s
That's still going strong, made of metal and glass
Where visitors to our town, surely won't want to pass
Take a stroll along the promenade, there are lots of things to see
And the people are so friendly, and kind as can be
Because you see, we live beside the sea.

Shirley-Patricia Cowan

The Lost Airfield

On a grey October day
To Kenley Airfield we made our way
As we drove through leaden light
We saw a most surprising sight
It stretched as far as we could see
Transported back in time were we.

Where two world wars have left their ghosts
The historic Earth was trod by hosts
Of men and women building planes
Then flying off in ordered skeins
With a loud distinctive roar
These aeroplanes flew far to war

The airfield is quiet now, only gliders fly
Soaring swiftly high so high
They silently, secretly glide through the air
The dog walkers below don't see or care.

The war memorial carved in stone
Three figures standing all alone
Look out on this nostalgic sight
Gleaming in the pale twilight.

We enjoyed our visit and yet
Wear scarlet poppies so we don't forget.

Valerie Coleman

To The Balcombe Dustmen

Who would be a dustman?
Well, I would for one.
We keep this village tidy
With humour, jokes and fun.
We are not only junkmen,
We're experts at our jobs.
If not for us this village,
If left unto the yobs,
Would soon revert to jungle
With broken glass, beer cans
And trash and litter everywhere,
Fag packets, all of Man's
Rubbish. Lazy throwaways!
The drop-it-at-you-feet
Mentality this generation
Is trying hard to beat.
If you good folks would do
Our job but for a week
You'd then appreciate
The pressing need to keep
The dogs and cats from ripping
Up the plastic sacks.
They try to get into
The bags for juicy snacks.
Who's worse?
The starving animal
Or thoughtless litter lout
Who chucks his rubbish over
His neighbour's hedge and shouts –
'Why does the local council
Not clean the village street?
It's their responsibility,
Not mine to keep things neat.'
We dustmen try to do
Our best to keep things sweet,
But don't expect the dustman
To clean under your feet.
If you would only do
Your bit to keep things clean
We'd soon become redundant
And Balcombe would be 'green'.

John McCall

In Epping Forest

Stroll through the woods
Find the remains of an ancient Roman camp.
Amongst the two hundred-year-old Beech trees.
Roman ramparts, now large Earth banks,
Where the gates used to be,
Empty spaces,
Overgrown by trees.
Badgers dug holes in the banks
To see the badgers, be up early to see.

A spring that feeds,
The little muddy stream,
I think, that where the Romans used to drink.
Real inspiring place.
Sunlight through hundred feet trees.
Like permanent twilight.
Sunbeams what are seen,
Filter down through the tall trees,
Is that a Roman soldier I see? Maybe!

Bryan G Clarke

The Post Office Tower

(For Walt Whitman)

Tubed by glass or maybe Perspex
standing, recalling past popular songs,
the too-tall awkward girl,
is still wearing too many sequins
at the party,
she, the shy one that nobody talks to.
If Whitman stood next to me now
I would tell him and he would understand,
'There she is, still here!
We shall not mock her or our being alive,
we shall not mock her singing old songs,
we shall not mock her revolving tiara,
for she is there, singing until dawn,
and we shall give thanks and applaud.'

Adam Campbell

LUTON OR DUNSTABLE

I love going to Luton Town
When I've time to look around.
There are goods galore
A good variety in every store.
Cafes for a snack or meal
Takeaways and a sandwich bar
Fresh baked bread and rolls
Catch a bus or go by car
Maybe a coach or train to go far.
There are pubs, clubs, library too
This busy town has lots to do.
There are public parks nearby
Ponds with ducks that fly.
Children's playgrounds for fun all around.

I love Dunstable too –
Not forgetting the nearby zoo.
There are fewer shops, but quality there
And open market and a craft fair.
Nice places if you want to eat
Seats around to rest your feet.
Pubs and discos to stay out late
Maybe there meet a date.
Here there's lots to do
Luton and Dunstable don't compare –
Either place, it's good there.

Sheila Waller

The Diamond Jubilee

The Diamond Jubilee of our dear Queen
She looked so beautiful and radiant as ever been,
And never had we seen people's face so bright
As they celebrated in the radiant sunlight.

With flags and buntings thousands prettily flying
The neighbourhood alights with friendly children singing,
The children all dressed up, they felt so merry
To see the tables all laden with food for their bellies.

With colours bright and high flying Union Jacks
All in the sunshine in their fashioned shirts and hats,
Flags in their hundreds and tablecloths were owned
By most courageous citizens from all over town.

But the Thames came to life with those flotillas
For several days like the gondolas,
Our dear Queen and Duke stood ahoy, they were strong;
On that bedecked barge for hours long.

The Queen's outfits were some super shades
Those colours blended so well the pale greens, the reds, the blues, the lilacs,
Meticulously chosen, her smile says a lot
God bless you and the Duke Ma'am and you are the tops.

Mary Joseph

Cissbury Ring

One day I looked to Cissbury Ring
And saw her smiling face
It seemed she was inviting me
To feel her fond embrace.

I ambled up the gentle path
That led me through the trees
The trees were all a'murmuring
Responding to the breeze.

Then when I reached the ancient ring
That overlooks the sea
The skylarks with their joyful song
Rose up to welcome me.

Just as an eagle on the heights
Surveys his chosen land
I felt a sense of freedom
From the countryside I scanned.

The Seven Sisters in the sun
Enjoyed the evening light –
Contrasting with the Sussex Weald –
A switchback gleaming white.

And looking west expectantly
Across the hills of baize
I glimpsed the bashful Isle of Wight
Veiled by a summer haze.

So if you're feeling down at heart
Then please take this advice
Go rest awhile on Cissbury Ring
And sample Paradise.

Jonathan Bryant

What Kent Has Meant

The flowers – the trees – the birds – the bees
Do come please – you will find Kent so exciting
Here in the 'old' – the 'new' – so much to view
As you will see as you stroll through villages inviting,
Here be a love that's truly awaiting you
The hop fields and the ploughing
Much to warm the heart e'er you do depart
I am so glad that Kent I am now in
We live happily – my family and me
With no more of sobbing
As quite by chance – our lives to enhance
We escaped the bombing
From London we sped, then all roads led
To Gillingham where we gained a welcome
Dodging that bad curse,
Coming home to nurse
My dear sweet wife's grandmum,
It has been great since –
No more need to wince
Instead the joy of living
They were bad times
With some evil crimes
That – perhaps one day we can be forgiving
Right now – this day – it's hip hip hooray
I'm an accepted in Kent new fighter
Trying hard to be what is expected of me.
To make afflicted's lives the brighter.
With others like self – left upon the shelf
Who are too – somewhat disabled
I'm doing all I can
As a 'garden of England' fan
To be as a 'man of Kent' too labelled
Here in Kent history reigns
It'll be in my veins forever –
I will stay put as I have taken root
I'll leave this haven – never!
It's not just sod –
It's cherished by god
As through it I plod – I love it
It's worth so much
Do stay in touch –
It's my golden nugget!

John Leonard Wright

Buckingham Fair

When Grandma went to Buckingham Fair,
She walked five miles through the country lanes
And she carried two sacks and a basket to cope,
And wished there was one of the new-fangled trains.

The annual Fair was an absolute must,
As there were no shops anywhere near,
So she filled her sacks with pots, brushes and pails
Which she hoped would suffice for the year.

Then back she trudged with her heavy pack,
Hoping perhaps for a lift in a cart,
And thinking, with guilt, of the brooch she had bought,
Shaped like an arrow piercing a heart.

When Mother went a few years later,
She drove herself in a pony and trap,
But the Fair had declined – far fewer booths.
Old faces were missing which left a large gap.

She still made a purchase of luxury goods,
Such as almonds, spices and soap,
And she looked at the horses and wished she could buy,
On a farmer's wife's pittance, there wasn't a hope.

Then after the war it was my turn to visit
And I pedalled my bike through the same country ways.
The Fair was much smaller with few things to buy.
I spent most of my time in the gun shooting bays.

I then had a go at the old hoopla stall
And I tried very hard at hooking a duck,
I did win a goldfish to put in my pond,
But aiming at darts was my one bit of luck.

My daughter now follows me; the Fair's changed again.
The old music has gone and just noise has replaced it.
The roundabouts, dodgems and slides are too fast,
So I only walk round and dream of the past.

I'm glad it's surviving; it's part of our heritage.
And too much of that has been frittered away.
So good luck to the Fair people; may they continue,
And hold fast to their fairground for many a day.

Elizabeth Zettl

Come And See London

Well London, what can I say?
Home to Big Ben which you can see from miles away
Tourist attractions such as Madame Tussaud's and the London Eye
My gosh, it's rather high.

Buckingham Palace guarded by man and horse
This is the home of her majesty the Queen of course
Home to exciting events such as the Queen's Diamond Jubilee
A celebration for millions to take part in and see.

The best place for an English cup of tea
With a scone or maybe strawberries with clotted cream
Home to fish and chips eaten on Friday nights
With people tucking in, enjoying every bite.

Home to the 2012 Olympics with the finest runners and swimmers
Home to the nation's Sunday dinner
All the family at the table talking, laughing and making a lot of noise
The brothers and sisters playing with their toys.

The London Underground, the fastest way to get around
It travels to all different places day or night
Such as the London Dungeons if you fancy a fright

Home to the Prime Minister at number ten Downing Street
You can walk round London for hours and hours if you don't mind aching feet
Getting in a taxi and taking in the views
Maybe going to Hyde Park to see a concert or two

Going out to museums, galleries and shops
You always end up buying lots and lots
Souvenirs, postcards, T-shirts and books
Then dining out in restaurants with the finest of cooks.

Places filled with cobbled streets and red telephone boxes
Horses pulling carriages, they're as strong as oxes
Famous landmarks such as the Gherkin and Westminster Abbey
All visited by the clocking of the cabbies.

The capital of England
The names for the Monopoly board game
People waving the England flags, their spirits high, that will never change
They're proud of their colours, the red, white and blue
They're proud of their country, and I am too.

Emily Hendy

Clacton-On-Sea, Our Star

Distant, the light seen again
Through skies sodden with weeping
Lovely – all signs of nature
Slowly – bright colours creeping.

Softly – birdsong – then higher
As more voices join choir
Welcome – the break of new day
That's what nature's heralds say.

Awesome – the sea, that temptress
Skirts swirling in winter storms
Alert mariners – watchful
Knowing sea in all its forms.

Today's gown is azure blue
Hiding folds of darker hue Gentle waves under pier lap
Leaving strand an untouched map.

Then the sun, that golden cask
Throws aside his facial mask –
Clifftop daffodils ignite
Yellow trumpets shining bright.

Some nights fireworks on pier
Show a glorious picture clear
Of Clacton – the sky – the sea
Happiness – for you – for me.

Ah but that is not the end –
Oh the fun we've had this week
As we our Queen and Philip thank
Happiness is at its peak
In Clacton – star of the east coast.

Daphne Young

Golden Green (In Kent)

This is where I live,
Nature's treat to hear the early morning cuckoo, echoing near, but out of sight,
The blackbird's song ringing out across the fields,
In clement weather you can see little birds foraging for food, twittering as they search.
Rabbits bobbing to and fro in the field across the road.
Sunlight gleaming through swaying branches, lighting up bluebells below.
Traffic passes unaware of their surrounds
A fox appears wandering as if no place to go, looking for a sunny spot to bask awhile undisturbed by human folks,
Such a beautiful creature maligned by many, saunters under shifting summer clouds.
Pigeons cooing, collecting twigs to line their nests within the eaves.
A robin so bold looks for worms when gardening comes to a close.
All this is nature's gift, if you listen, wait, watch and see
The freshly planted corn waits to ripen before a storm.
A balloon passes across the sky, destination unknown, slowly disappears in the evening glow.
You may be lucky and hear the geese,
They fly high in formation, a sight to please the eye.
Be aware if you should came this way,
So much is hidden but is surely there
Nature's bounty held in store in Golden Green.

Liz Dicken

A Royal Park

Springtime flowers peep at the sky,
Awoken by the birds that once sang them a lullaby.
Each daffodil a yellow that's greeted by the sun,
Their golden unique beauty is imitated by each one.
A variety of colours stand, the polyanthus bright
The abundant crocuses are a truly triumphant sight.
Across this hilly grassland spreads a luxury of flowers,
Resembling a homemade carpet of threaded woollen flowers.
God's tapestry is laid till the summer months to come
When He'll change His fertile needle with colours newly strung.
Squeezing drops of rain are some friendly passing clouds,
Formed From God's golden pipe to watch over all His flowers.
Refreshing those that woke to a day of regal mise
Into this royal park they are seen by admiring eyes.

Sandra Brisck

DELAYED VISION

(A satire)

Wordsworth tells us – as a boy
Lakeland's bounty was his joy. His mind's mate a nature queen
Monarch of the virgin scene.
His lady threatened the stolen boat
As he struggled with guilt
And to keep afloat.
Struck on the oar – to row
Lest sink in spontaneous overflow.

He set off Nutting with his crook
Through happy dell and one dear nook.
Striking at the banquet feast,
As some wild audacious beast.
Guilt again – at ravaged goods
Defiling the spirit of the woods.

But wait a minute – where is this bliss?
I don't remember half of this,
With powerful feelings
And faithful friend
This prelude paradox
Must surely end.

For I was a Lakeland fellow too.
Later yes, but does it start anew?
Were winters then half as nifty
As they were in nineteen-fifty?
Dear old Will recalls daffodils
While I remember tiresome hills.

Hills indeed – and dingy dells,
Rocky crags, misty fells, and hidden hollows
That snared you as you chased the swallows.
Nettles that clung at arms and knees
And the smell of sheep on the breeze.

No glasslike mere with surface satin.
'Goodness me! What have I sat in?'
I, like the Homebound Labourer stalk,
And everywhere an upward walk – but
Wait again – am I unkind?
Perhaps Will is right, it's in the mind.

Is it for this I reminisce?
Did I sleep, or just resist
This vision I see? – A willow
Strewing down to dewy mist
By mossy stream – like amethyst.
'Oh Will it's true! Now I see
recollected for me in tranquillity.'

Leonard Watson

This City Of The Crows

London, the city of the crows,
Those black forms scavenging
Where the concrete wind grimly blows –
Crows cackle, do not sing,

And London has no melody;
It whines, it grinds, it lacks a soul –
Ugly as a crow, it must be
This hell, this starkness, this cruel hole

In which we struggle, on Tube trains,
Down streets, and then I see once more
A crow's beak stabbing out the brains
Of a doomed man all smeared with gore.

London – nightmare – crows in a crowd.
I hear them always, wild and loud . . .

Zekria Ibrahimi

LANE END – A CHILTERN VILLAGE

Lane End, sits there
Between two peaks
Finings to the west
Park Wood to the east.

Look to the south, a castle see
Home of the Windsors our royalty
To the north, to the Three Ends
A part of us and homes of friends.

A lofty place, atop its hill
The winds can howl, the rains can spill
But all who are here, must agree
'Tis quite a place to live and be.

Its history is written well
Yet annals never can foretell
Just what the future years will bring
But one thing's sure, the birds will sing.

Timbered woods create our bounds
Where ash and oak and beech are found
Patchwork commons, and meadows green
A sight for all, it must be seen.

A working village, Lane End is
Diversified, cross sections biz
Farmer, blacksmith, water refine
Butcher, baker, chairs that recline.

Injected plastic, graphic art
A long way since the horse and cart
The orient are now mine host
Where Temperance, was the once proud boast.

A school demolished, now conference centre
Japanese learn from English mentor
But we enjoy its golfer's greens
And heated pool, behind glass screens.

Lane End has changed, and will again
Progress, forward, there's slight restraint
Expanding here, developing there
Planners please, you must take care.

The churches, chapel, village hall
Educate, and serve us all
The pubs create, part social life
Places now, to take your wife.

Lane End has multiplied her acres
Dwellings now, where we were players
Some of us packed trunk and left
To the north, east, south and west
But you all know, you're welcome back
Just down the *lane,* at *end* of track.

Trevor Perrin

THE CHILTERN HILLS

The Chiltern, Chiltern, Chiltern Hills,
There is golden wheat and windmills,
Hopefully, they'll stay forever,
But chalky, flinty soils wherever!

In spring, the beechwoods rise all blue.
At dawn the meadows soaked in dew
We visit them; resource the earth,
Where mushrooms spring for cooking worth.

The ancient whitethorn fills our hedges,
Willows, limes amongst the sedges
Makes a contrast with the greens;
High lands, low lands, all beauty scenes.

Canals and rivers, marshlands few,
With sailing boats and Whipsnade Zoo.
We've stately homes, sweet villages,
There's rapeseed crops for tillages.

Churches old, now theatres new,
Pubs, museums, vineyards too.
Public footpaths, cycle tracks,
Deer in parks, escaped muntjacs.

In green-banked lanes, we walk ahead,
Where tree-leaves tunnel overhead.
We've sports of all kinds, even bowls.
The Chilterns now are in our souls.

R Wilson

1066 COUNTRY

Living in London for forty-five years
with the hustle and bustle in my youth
they were not happy times I remember quite clear
I dreamed of peace and quiet, with friends to share
But that was never to be, I fear!
As the years went by, an my life seemed dull
I could see no future, I was in a mull!
I now had two sons, what the future for them?
Things were getting worse, and I could not stay
I simply had to get away!
Then came the day, I was offered a change
To East Sussex, my life to rearrange
I came here in 1969, and never looked back
The peace and quiet of this beautiful town
With countryside and trees and flowers
Seaside views and God's own showers
All things created by His mighty hand!
My future was now looking grand.
I now have a home, with lovely things
And all the blessings that He alone brings
Thank you Lord for my lovely home
And for bringing me here, no more to roam!

Miss Terry Thompson

Southend

Southend, Southend,
Is where I want to be,
Under the sun, on the sand, by the sea.
Rows of beach huts side by side,
Sails billowing, boats bobbing
On the morning tide,
People walking along the seafront,
Children enjoying the adventure playground,
Whoops of joy, screaming, shouting
Summer is here!
Casinos for gambling day and night,
Fish and chips – a typical sight,
Rossi's ice cream kiosks to the left and right.
And Pier Hill is new,
And the longest pier – wonderful to view.
Southend has lots to see and do.
Come and visit for a day – it's not a long way.
Southend will welcome you.

Mary Jo Clayton

Morning Bliss

I wake up in the morning with a smile on my face,
The sun is shining brightly, the birds tweeting away.
So I travel to work, with a song in my heart,
A beautiful day it seems, until I walk through the door,
My feet feeling heavy, my surrounding is so cramped,
The noise getting louder and my ear drum thumping fast.

I asked myself a question, why did I get out of bed?
But a soft voice came back to me,
At least you're still alive!
So I look at my surroundings and think how lucky I am,
My body may be aching, my ear drum ready to burst
But still I'm almost standing, if only for a while.

The time is ticking slowly now, it's almost time to go
To take a well-earned rest from this humdrum noisy place.
So I gather up my finished jobs, put them in their rightful place,
And quickly make my way through the exit door.
Now homeward bound I go, the sun still shining brightly,
Another day has come and gone, who knows what tomorrow will bring.

Elane Jackson

To Sissinghurst

I came to Sissinghurst today
And wandered through its garden rooms,
Each one a feast of sight and smell,
Laid like a carpet round the red-bricked tower,
From which the verdant countryside is viewed.
In spring the bluebells form a haze
Beneath the Kentish cobnut trees,
While in the cottage garden blaze
The reds and golds in glorious profusion.
Each garden hidden by its hedge of yews
Forming its sculptured boundary
Reveals a fresh delight before my eyes.
As darkness falls white flowers glow,
Eerily beautiful to see,
While scents profuse delight from herbs
Planted in their own special place.
Purple and white wisteria hangs
And roses ramble on these ancient walls.

Garden of mystery, garden of beauty,
Created with such love and toil
By Vita Sackville-West, poet and novelist,
Bringing to this neglected spot in Kent
Her happy memories of Knowle
Whose lovely gardens were the setting
For her more youthful years.
Set amidst rolling countryside with placid moat
Sissinghurst glows – a glorious scented legacy
For all to now enjoy.

Roma Davies

THE GARDEN

As I lie in the garden drowsing
Enjoying the sun's healing rays,
It seems that I hear fairy music
The flowers are singing their lays.

The small rockery plants are humming
Summer air is alive with song,
The lovely trees have deeper voices
Birds trill as they fly along.

Such a beautiful spot is a garden
It is the happiest place I know.
Nearest God's heart and I take delight
In helping His creations grow.

I talk to the trees as to brothers
All flowers are my little friends
I bid them be good children and bloom
How I miss them when summer ends.

What would life be without a flower
A bird's song, a humming bee
Or trees with apples ripening there?
And the best things in life are free.

Elizabeth Elcoate-Gilbert

Looking Closer

Look out for the homeless
They do us no harm
They may be on street corners
No place to keep warm
They may carry a burden
Of which you don't know
Look into their faces
I'm sure it will show
Behind their old clothing
Is one in disguise
With many a sad tale
Your see in their eyes
They need our support
To carry them through
I dare to be in their shoes
Would you?

Dorothy Morley

The Place Where I Live

Detached houses all around
Prosperity states its name
I live poor – cocooned by wealth
From outside looks the same.

A tiny room, a lifetime's trove
It's where I lay my head
No shiny car gleams on my drive
A Freedom Pass instead.

Yet through my kitchen glass I spy
A robin eat his tea
A bowl of seeds upon the lawn
Placed lovingly by me.

And all my neighbours' riches fade
Into obscurity
The birds, the trees, the peace and quiet
Make this place heavenly.

S J Kattenburg

Chiltern Charms

Winds on crisp autumn days send red and gold leaves whirling,
Creating crackling carpets; see smoke signals curling.
On Chiltern Hills in wintertime, landscape's white aglow,
Freezing, frozen, frosty fingers, falling snow!

Little villages hideaway among Chiltern Hills
Winding rivers weave their way amid swift flowing rills.
Old school houses still standing surrounded by tall trees
Children's ringing laughter floating on the breeze.

In springtime discovering new lambs skipping gaily
Sensing warm sunshine bringing fragrant blossoms daily.
On Chiltern Hills in summer, a bright blue cloudless sky,
Reflections in the rivers; boats gliding by.

Chiltern Hills stand overlooking valleys deep and dales
Watch, as the sun sends a beam sweeping across the vales
Majestic clouds in the sky, seeming close to Heaven
Strata cumulus; promised rainbow given.

Then, follow the trail of a jet plane high in the blue
Glimpsing a skylark winging the carefree course she flew.
Chiltern Hills, breathe in clear air, freshening, uplifting
Cobwebs disappear; rolling clouds go drifting.

Sheep and cattle gently graze in rural pastures green
Turning heads around to gaze upon the peaceful scene.
Chiltern churches welcoming – steeple bells peal, ringing
Calling folk to worship, joyful singing.

Tiny cottages abound with pretty gardens neat.
A sleepy cat curls upon a rustic garden seat.
Leafy woodlands sheltering; gorse, bramble on the heath,
Birds sing from a hawthorn, building nests beneath.

Country towns on market days as bustling shoppers seek
Among brightly coloured stalls the bargains of the week.
Bridges spanning riverbanks, there's boating on a lake,
Fishing from the river, cycling, hikes, partake.

You would not guess whilst wandering among Chiltern scenes
Just over yonder hillsides are motorway machines.
Towns are being modernized with indoor shopping malls
Sports facilities and ten screen movie halls.

Chiltern villages retaining views of rural life
Life with slower pace seems to bring freedom from strife.
The world goes on rushing by and problems just increase
Yet within the Chilterns, find places of peace.

Joan Heybourn

Royal Connections (2012)

What a joy,
What a pride
To know
That we are at the heart
Of the Diamond Jubilee Celebrations!

The south London street,
On which our castle-like house,
High and large stands,
Boasts about its fame:

Shares its name
With the royal regalia that played
A main part at Queen's Coronation!

On June the 3rd,
Fifty-nine years to the day,
An orb in her right hand
The Queen held.

That jewelled globe meant
To indicate,
That as the Head
Of both State and Anglican Church,
She was keen to defend
The hearth and altar of the realm!

Lucy Carrington

Anglia Our Pride

As the rainbow of your Eastern skies, arcs her beauty round
While the first rains of springtime, fall on fens and open ground
In wonder at your serenity, we will listen to your sound,
And for the beauty which is Anglia, we will remember you.

Stretching wide your creeks and fenlands, kissed by banks of snow,
The majesty of your windswept rushes, sets our hearts aglow,
Peaceful rivers make their journey, from broads down to the sea,
Carrying home your beauty, once again to me.

As snow falls upon your lowlands, without the slightest sound,
With swirling mists moving, quietly all around,
Stillness is in the air, a white carpet on the ground,
Setting our spirits once more afire, and a pride within abounds.

Warmly blow your eastern breezes, sweeping over the land,
Writing many patterns like a hidden hand,
Your swirling mists give way, revealing sapphire skies of blue
For the beauty that is Anglia, we will remember you.

Proud stands your reeds and rushes, rising very high,
Twilight is falling now, painting a darkness in the sky,
As those last tides of autumn, flow gently over sand,
They reveal again the nature and beauty of our land.

With hills sloping downwards, and climbing up again,
A stirring in the wind, rustles through wheat and grain,
From villages, hamlets, towns and farms too,
For folk who work and till the land, what they see is true.

Fresh ripplings on the Broads, as the wind sweeps around,
The furthest star above us, is brightly shining down,
For all Anglian peoples, wherever they abide,
The beauty which is East Anglia, is our homeland and our pride.

Jim Wilson

At Twilight Time

There's a certain beauty, on a winter's day,
With twilight near, a chill breeze at play,
A-rustling and tussling, last greenery to thrive,
The birds flying homewards, a hope to survive,
A smattering of snow o'er the lawn and sloping eaves,
The sheltering hedgerows still sporting leaves,
To nurture them with some semblance of care,
how, with sunlight fast fading, I sit and stare
And marvel at God's purpose, His heavenly plan,
Set in place when our world began.

I am carried far away, to another realm
And feel contentment, with God at the helm,
For He moves with the frailty of moving things,
With the strength of the sun, on golden wings,
He breathes on Earth, in all manner of ways
And alters the seasons to suit all our days,
He can sow living hope into every soul –
And, with loving arms, make a person whole,
When hearing our troubled minds, He presides –
For all who will listen – He alone resides.

At twilight time, when all is still –
Take His outstretched hand – He will fulfil.

Julia Eva Yeardye

Sunday Walk – The Canal, Little Venice

Faces bear tracks, drooping lines around the mouth.
    A landscape of caps, cigarettes, littered streets.
       The wind snatches at your umbrella.
The current sucks it down into the canal water,
    like a mischievous child.
Women shake mats, their men cut the grass.
Fish bait lies in wait in wooden containers.

We shelter beneath coal-black rafters
    where pigeons conspire and
    then dance along the towpath
     to memories of old musicals and
     drink sweet tea in a café,
Its walls covered in red and gold mock velvet.

    The dusky owner hits the jackpot,
smilingly inserts more coins into the fruit machine.
    Five Chinese dishes are served.
    Mukesh's eyes glimmer with a rare beauty.
We discuss Gandhi, mixed marriages, the Russian pipeline.
    Father is serene, forgets past prejudices.
    There is integration in a new land.

    Sensing love, the rain is gentler now.

Sandra Eros

On A Cornish Sunday

(A memoir from my life and times in the West Country)

On a Cornish Sunday in the morning when the sunshine
still half-red and barely gold is fresh from its beginning,
I follow down the river's course; it shrinks from spate to trickle
diminishing before the great and restless open sea

The mewling cry of seabirds mingles with the sound of engines
and the smoky rainbow sea haze rises up to meet the hillsides,
catching in its airborne droplets, and carrying it landwards,
the smack of salty ozone from the ocean's endless tides

He's coming now, the fish man, with his crabs, their heavy armour
red-boiled on the barrow; heavy-pincered and crook-legged,
menacing, but done for, bound for tourist salads;
small parts of the harvest yielded up by summer seas

Down here among the shop fronts, weary with the weight of wares,
seashells, rock and postcards, novelties (no batteries),
stand the out-of-towners, steeped in local colour,
browsing through the pastures of the village thoroughfares

John Varrick in the tavern, arms like legs of mutton,
tattooed with an anchor and a heart enclosing 'Mother',
serving pints and chasers, pauses from his labours,
squints towards the sunlight as it falls across the floor

In the afternoon writing postcards on the beacon,
I watch the glinting ships as they flirt with far horizons,
bid them fond goodbye though I never really knew them,
try to touch the seagulls though they're halfway out to sea

Finally the evening, smoulder after swelter,
finely cut with breezes where the sun has dropped its guard,
slot machines and cafés, their lights are stealing lustre
from the daylight as it ebbs below the promenade

Tony Crawford

Not Mugged Yet

Seventy-three . . . with
shrivelled muscles, sagging flesh.
Timid. Patronised.
Am I safe here?

annual pension
average. Life-time savings
lose value daily.
Am I safe here?

Threats to seize assets
delivered two days after
their tax has been paid.
Am I safe here?

Plain-clothed marksmen, told
to tail a 'terrorist', kill
the brown-skinned suspect.
Am I safe here?

A cold-caller brow-
beats me into disclosing
an account number.
Am I safe here?

Terrorist attacks?
Guided missile batteries
placed in local parks.
Am I safe here?

Loud knocks at the door.
Two men in day-glo vests ask
to cut down my trees.
Am I safe here?

A helicopter,
vigilantes and police.
Rioters looting.
Am I safe here?

The National
Health Service privatized soon?
Punished if you're poor?
Am I safe here?

Fewer crossings and
less time for pedestrians.
Cyclists on footpath.
Am I safe here?

Stuck with expensive
stamps, my Royal Mail package
slit open . . . emptied.
Am I safe here?

Mike Cleary

The Joys Of Epping Forest

The Hollow Pond, surrounded by a fringe
Of verdant forest, stretches in a copse
Of glistening water live with snow-white swans –
A lake of azure calm reflecting skies
Of clouding grey or deep cerulean blue.
Amidst its shallows rise green islands dense
With woodland – forest miniatures as lush
As Asian jungles. Beyond the pond itself
Lies an open meadow, once the home
Of soaring skylarks, now a grassy plain
Interspersed with freshly budding willows –
Home to multicoloured butterflies.

Around the Hollow Pond swell golden banks
Alive with stunted oaks whose hoary trunks
Are canopied with foliage. A belt
Of virgin forest tangled with the roots
Of countless trees winds up and down the humps
And creeks of the sheltered pond. Here oaken aisles
Of sylvan splendour flank a rising bank
Where once the Lido lay – a swimming pool
Encircled by green forest. As of old,
Cyclists ride and jump the sloping knolls
While boaters on the lake punt and splash
Around the islands in their hired canoes.

The forest stretches south and north: first south
To the wide expanse of Wanstead Flats, then on
To Bush Wood – a bewitching labyrinth
Of crossing footpaths girt by ornate walls
Of oaks festooned with holly. Wanstead Park,
Graced by Heronry Pond, gives way to shrubs
And bushes – Scouting territory rife
With gorse and hawthorn brakes. Farther north
Forest Rise ascends with swathes of grass
Towards St Peter's Church. Here a maze
Of oaken glades soon opens out to where
The Rising Sun Pond, nestling deep

Within a meadow ringed by ancient oaks,
Flowers with rushes, reeds and lily pads
Around a jungle island. Sylvan shades
Reach out to Woodford, Chingford and beyond;
And Bury Wood, which crosses Chingford Plain,
Forms oaken avenues where Cuckoo Brook

Winds its way through labyrinths of trees.
Epping Forest broadens out to Loughton,
Beyond which its northernmost reaches –
Wintry Wood and the Lower Forest –
Wind through Thornwood Common, on to Ware
In Hertfordshire. But Loughton boasts the best

Of Epping Forest, for here, in Monk Wood,
Oaks give way to beeches; here deep dells
With velvet greenswards fed by cool springs –
Labyrinthine streams with moss-grown banks –
Slope in emerald lawns to wooded bowers
Where hornbeam avenues and beechen groves
Overhang with drooping canopies
And leafy arbours. Here, the very heart
Of Epping Forest borders on a mead,
Deershelter Plain, where fallow fawns
Still thrive. This woodland paradise resounds
To purest strains from song thrush, nightingale

And blackbird. Robins, blackcaps and a host
Of finches, chats and warblers soon join in.
The song of Epping Forest never ceases,
Echoing angelic choirs above.
Glory, praise and honour to the One
Whose word sustains Creation, and whose love
And power reign throughout eternity
In Heaven above and on the Earth below.
Give praise to God – Creator, Lord and Saviour,
To God the Father, Son and Holy Ghost,
To God the Three in One and One in Three
Now and for evermore. Amen.

Robert D Hayward

Sydenham – Once Ken, Now London, SE26

How Sydenham has changed during my lifetime.
I was born here in 1920.
There were fields then nearby –
Some with cows and sheep, feeding on the grass.
Gardens had chickens, and grew their own vegetables
Fresh fish was sold at the door, a fishmonger
Walked around the streets with a box of
Fresh fish on his head, brought up that morning
From the coast.
The baker came around with bread baked
Locally, and meat was killed in Penge.
Cattle were taken to the abattoir behind
The pub and killed in the yard.
Rabbits were hung outside the butchers' shops
And when sold, the fur was stripped off them,
And sold to furriers to make coats,
And the backing for winter gloves.
Nothing was wasted then.
Fruit was grown in the gardens.
There were plenty of apples, pears, plums,
Cherries, mulberries, all various varieties.
So there was no shortage, as surplus food
Was given to churches and organisations
To distribute it. There were always volunteers.
Sydenham was a country area, and a
Pleasant local place situated near London.
A village. Lower Sydenham came with the
gas works, and the canal, and Upper Sydenham
Was where many big land owners settled.
After the Crystal Palace was built, and they
Employed local people to build it.
I grew up in this area. There were small
Local schools, usually run by one or two
Maiden ladies – children learned to read
Write, spell and add up. In the winter we
All sat around an open coal fire.

Life was much simpler then, you could
Trust people and churches were very active.
There were rules of behaviour, and if you
Didn't behave you were punished.
The big change came with World War Two
1939-45 – after this everything altered.
Men came back changed, women went out to work.
Home life altered.
Prices rose everywhere, and more
Money had to be found.
Sydenham was not the same.
I think I am the oldest local inhabitant
As I still lived only five minutes away from the
House where I was born. Ninety-two years ago.

Doris E Pullen

Sanctuary

Where the secret waters hide
Under temperamental sky,
Swans, supremely lovely, glide;
Do they, reincarnated, cry
Of former man or bird or beast,
Forsaken dreams of chafing ploy,
Craving surrounds of our south-east
In which to paint resplendent joy?
Who can feasibly surmise
When and if, since alien clime,
Past souls severed western ties
To taste and smell our summertime?
Watching by Carshalton Ponds,
I feel how satisfied they seem,
Great white saints by fragile fronds,
Softening Surrey colours scheme.
Stately they pass, cool, remote
Whilst, forever a dreamer, I
Seeing them serenely float,
Ask myself if such grace could die,
Omnipotence intervene
To prove, where humble ripples greet,
That a guiding hand has been
To sanction one south-east retreat.

Ruth Daviat

ENFIELD

Within the outskirts of Northern London,
Where we can find, half-country, part-town,
There's a place named Enfield
Where men and beasts abound.

Many years ago, in olden days,
Enas Field, was its name,
And even now remains the choice
Where Elizabeth the First, gave it fame.

However in later years, came a cloud,
Declaring war to those below,
Sirens sounded very loud,
Menacing raids brought a horrible blow.

Ration books become the norm,
Munitions factory stood close by,
'Dig for Victory' placards shown,
encouraging people to have a try.

My father complied, grew his own,
I accompanied him one day to spy,
Hundreds of gliders above us did drone,
Carrying military to fight or die.

Soldiers billeted near our school,
Helped their comrades preparing meals,
'Stay in the shelter' was the rule
'Until the all clear siren' peals.

Without a warning, a flying bomb,
Sent by foe, stopped overhead,
A loud explosion, our hope gone,
School, soldiers, shelter, nothing spared.

In happier days I watched with friends,
As 'Enfield Cardinals' baseball played
An American game to bring amends,
With English buddies, friendships made.

Habits changed for Enfield folk,
Riding on buses, no longer norm,
Owning a car, a fervent hope,
To scour the district until dawn.

Tower blocks began to rise,
Changing the skyline for those below,
Work became constant with cash applied,
Ambitious hopes began to grow.

A faster pace has changed the world,
Including Enfield, which does the same
I've lived here proudly, since a girl
Between the sunshine and the rain.

Margaret Nicholl

LIKE A PHOENIX

London is a special place,
A magnet for the human race,
A history book, not finished yet,
It is one place we can't forget.

What history that she could tell,
We've had our strife, but bore it well,
The Great Fire of London took us down,
Like a phoenix rose a greater town.

And like a beacon, shining high,
St Paul's Cathedral touches the sky,
A testimony to the brave,
It still has many more souls to save.

A symbol of hope amidst the Blitz
When all around was crushed in bits
St Paul's Cathedral stood her ground
And gave us hope for miles around.

And Londoners are a special breed,
The city gives us all we need,
The royal parks, the stately homes
That only royalty has known.

The London culture is unique,
From all the languages that people speak,
And the diverse religions that abound
No greater city can be found.

Phoebe Brooks

Wild And Loved

What's special about my region?
Well I will tell you what is special,
We are a region of pet lovers,
Especially dogs and cats.

The dogs have grand personalities,
And are good company.
If you have a dog in the house,
A burglar will think twice!

And cats will catch and slice mice,
With paws and claws,
Devouring them with hungry jaws,
Then you will have a rodent problem no more!

The downside is dogs bark at every little thing,
Radios, phones, birds and noisy doorbells,
Will send them incessantly crazy,
And always wakes the baby!

Cats are not usually as loud as dogs,
But they have their moments too,
Eating the pet fish,
Or out of food dishes,
Set for your dinner parties,
Sneaky carts are very cheeky,
When it comes to food stealing.

We love them all the same,
Because we enjoy looking after them,
And we find their odd ways comical,
So bless every one of them.

Ali Sebastian

LONDON

London, dear London, the best place on Earth
I should know, it's the place of my birth,
Streets all full of treasures for all to savour
They sell nice ice creams too, in every flavour.
Wonderful buildings, hundreds of years old
Not these new glass things, they leave me cold.
If Christopher Wren saw that blooming Shard
He's be disgusted, he would take it quite hard.
Follow the Thames right down to the embankment
There's so much to see, so much entertainment
Wonderful bridges, statues and the like
Can't walk that far, you can ride Boris' bike.
Lovely green parks full of flowers and lakes
Cafés and restaurants selling tea, coffee and cakes,
Wherever you wander you'll find something new
Churches all open so you can sit in a pew,
Markets and shops selling nice souvenirs
Mind you the price will make you shed tears.
You can sit on the steps and listen to Big Ben
Near Parliament, supposedly filled with wise men,
Or go on a boat ride down to the Tower
No you don't have to row now, it's got engine power.
The Tower of London, now there's a place
That Bloody Tower will make your heart race,
If lucky you may get a glimpse of Anne Boleyn
With her head tucked under her arm, rattling a tin.
Just try it, a trip, up to Old London Town
You'll come back smiling, not wearing a frown,
This history, the stories and the happy smiling faces
You will agree with me it's the best of all places.

Dorothy Fuller

Dirty Old Town

I was born in 1930,
The year Wall Street go dirty
At age of three, at parents' knee,
Adolf Hitler came to tea, courtesy of the BBC.

My oldest friend, the Rev Stokes,
One of London's diamond blokes,
A fun guy, rather tall,
Was born behind the Salmon E Ball.

In Bethnal Green of salad days,
At Valance road there lived the Krays
And as the world went round the bend,
We moved to leafy Ponders End.

When I was ten the bombers came
Things would never be the same
Every night the hun returned,
For weeks on end the city burned.

The war deprived the land of wealth
Yet afterwards came the National Health.

Bill Looker

Neighbours In London

Neighbours in London sometimes are, the best or the worst you could see
Often making their presence felt, sometimes too noisy for me,
My neighbours are known by all, always know when they are home
We see the police and know they are back from wherever they roam.

My neighbours had a party, it lasted for four long days
They must have invited everyone, we hope it's just a phase,
The music was playing day and night, and lots of stamping feet
It felt like the world and its wife had come right next door to meet.

This party was so popular, and guests there was no limit
Partying all the time, not being quiet for one minute.
It seemed like there were thousands, the most I have ever seen
And this I really should expect as my neighbour is the Queen.

Irene Carroll

Easter 2012, Regent's Park

Shy willows hide their nakedness in green
Trembling as wanton breezes lift each ribboned tress;
Wavelets disturb the mirrors at their feet.

Still in their wintry mode the stoic oaks
Lift rugged elbows to the azure sky,
Their scourge-defying limbs
Point dark accusing fingers, stabbing high:
Come do your worst! Our leaves will live again!

Trees from Japan, white blossoms level-tiered,
Welcome the passing wanderers, like courtesans,
Beneath their snowy covers:
Wide open arms.

While herons, trim in black and white cravats,
(Fringed, most untidily, below their chests),
Proudly disdain the proffered flying crumbs,
As if they wait in ill-assembled ranks
The end-of-term photographer – to catch
Forever one fine passing day
Before the chores of adulthood
Exert their sway.

Frances Searle

Forward Poetry Information

We hope you have enjoyed reading this book - and that you will continue to enjoy it in the coming years.

If you like reading and writing poetry drop us a line, or give us a call, and we'll send you a free information pack.

Alternatively if you would like to order further copies of this book or any of our other titles, then please give us a call or log onto our website at www.forwardpoetry.co.uk

Forward Poetry Information
Remus House
Coltsfoot Drive
Peterborough
PE2 9BF
(01733) 890099